THE
COMPLETE
CHICKEN

CARL JEROME

THE COMPLETE CHICKEN

WINE NOTES BY
MARGARET STERN

ILLUSTRATIONS BY
PAT STEWART

RANDOM HOUSE
NEW YORK

Library of Congress Cataloging in Publication Data
Jerome, Carl.
The complete chicken.
Includes index.
1. Cookery (Chicken) I. Title.
TX750.J47   641.6'7'54   78–57141
ISBN 0–394–42822–6

Manufactured in the United States of America
2 4 6 8 9 7 5 3
First Edition

to
J. A. B.
and
J. G. S.

Poultry is for the cook
what canvas is for a painter . . . ; it is served
to us boiled, roasted, fried, hot or cold, whole or cut up, with
or without sauce, boned, skinned, stuffed,
and always with equal success.

BRILLAT-SAVARIN,
The Physiology of Taste
(translated by M. F. K. Fisher)

ACKNOWLEDGMENTS

--- ❖❖❖ ---

I'VE DEDICATED THIS BOOK to James Beard and John Simpson, which is my fullest expression of thanks to them—to James for his steadfast belief in my abilities, for his incredible patience in training me to understand and appreciate food and cooking, and for his affection and friendship; to John for the day-to-day support and encouragement he gave me during the eighteen months of testing and writing this book. My affection and appreciation are also due to Barbara Kafka for her friendship and for her ideas, particularly since the idea to do a book "just on chicken" was Barbara's. In addition, I would like to thank Morris Galen, Tom Margittai, and the late Helen McCully for their advice and friendship; Marion Cunningham, for that and much more; and Margaret Stern for the tremendous energies and effort that went into the wine notes.

Special thanks go to John Baily and Son, 116 Mount Street, London, W.1, England, my poulterer, who provided all of the chickens used to test this book; and in particular to the shop's owner, Mr. Derek, for answering my unending questions about the raising, rearing, and processing of chickens.

I also wish to thank Gail Winston, my editor, for pulling this book into shape, and Pat Brayne, my typist.

Finally, I can say little more by way of thanks and appreciation than to acknowledge that without the patient advice and guidance of my literary agent, Robert Lescher, and his wife, Susan, this book would not be.

C. J.
London

CONTENTS

INTRODUCTION

———— ❖❖❖ ————

WHEN I BEGAN writing this book, a friend said to me, "If I could eat only one meat for the rest of my life, it would be chicken." After testing several hundred recipes for this book—eating chicken more or less exclusively for eighteen months—I would have to agree: If I could choose only one meat for the rest of my life, it would indeed be chicken. Nutritionally, chicken is one of the best foods available—high in protein, and low in both calories and cholesterol. It is also one of the most widely available and least expensive meats. Gastronomically, chicken is incredibly versatile. No other meat adapts so well to so many different types of cooking—roasting, broiling, grilling, poaching, braising, fricasseeing, stewing, sautéing, frying, baking, to mention only a few. In addition, there are thousands of different combinations of ingredients and seasonings which can be used to complement and flatter the simple and delicious flavor and texture of a chicken. This book only skims the surface of the chicken's culinary possibilities.

As the manuscript for this book developed it began to take on its own character, and it became as much a book about cooking as a book about chicken. The chapters are divided by cooking techniques, not by courses. Chapters 1 and 2 deal with dry-cooking techniques—roasting, broiling, and grilling; Chapter 3 with moist cooking—everything from boiling to fricasseeing and stewing; and so on, through Chapter 10, which includes all of the technical matters relating to chicken—how to truss a chicken or bone a breast.

The chapter introductions explain in an easy-to-understand way the theory behind each technique. Following the theory section is a carefully detailed master recipe which shows how to apply the principles explained in the introduction. Once you understand the basic cooking techniques, all of the recipes are just variations on a theme. Therefore, if you can make a basic chicken fricassee, you can easily switch around a few ingredients and make a Country Captain or a Coq au Vin.

Always remember that there is only one absolute in cooking: There are no absolutes in cooking! The directions and explanations, and even the occasional proscription, are only guides to better cooking. They are not meant to imply that *this* is the only way to fry, or that *that* is the only way to sauté. Essential to good cooking is a clear understanding of the basic techniques. Home cooking does not demand the perfection in detail that *haute cuisine* does, but the more understanding you have of the details of fine cooking, the better your food will taste. If there is any question in your mind about a direction or what something means, read through the chapter introduction and the master recipe for that technique.

Good cooking does not require hours and hours in the kitchen. Far from it. With a little organization and forethought, almost every recipe in this book can be made with less than half an hour of actual preparation time—everything from the simplest, plain roast chicken for a family meal to the grand, elegant, and extravagantly expensive truffled French masterpiece, *poulet demi-deuil*.

Immediately following most recipes are menu or vegetable suggestions, as well as wine notes. These are only casual suggestions, for there is no need to serve two vegetables with every dinner nor, for that matter, to drink wine if you're not in the mood for it. Often you will find variations listed at the bottom of a recipe. These are not afterthoughts but ways of creating a whole new dish by varying just an ingredient or two. In addition, some of the recipes are followed by a paragraph about small changes that can be made. Cooking is and should be an individual and creative experience . . . go on, throw some tarragon in with the parsley and see what happens.

GENERAL INFORMATION ABOUT CHICKEN

TYPES OF CHICKEN

In the early part of this century you could still order a Rhode Island Red if you wanted a chicken for frying, or a Buff Orpington if you intended to poach it. Today's chickens have been "design bred," and although there may be slight differences from one company to another, for all intents and purposes a chicken is a chicken is a chicken. Buy chickens by weight, not by name, unless you want a fowl—that is, an old hen or cock for boiling —or a capon.

SMALL CHICKENS: The youngest chickens available, though they are expensive and often difficult to obtain, weigh from ¾ to 1¼ pounds. These tiny birds are more tender and juicy than their older brothers and sisters, and make beautiful individual servings. Split down the back, they are ideal broiled or grilled; they are excellent roasted whole, and they can be poached beautifully. (They are sometimes called squab or baby chickens, and are what the French refer to as *poussin.*)

MEDIUM-SIZED CHICKENS: Chickens weighing from 2 to 3 pounds are about two months old. They are tender, moist, and not very flavorful. These have become our "all-purpose" chicken—good for broiling or grilling, sautéing and frying, roasting, poaching, baking, casseroling, and fricasseeing. (At times they are labeled "broilers," "fryers," and "broiler-fryers.")

LARGE CHICKENS: Chickens weighing from 3 to 5½ pounds are three to four months old and are almost always called "roasters." They are not as juicy as the younger, medium-sized birds (which means they will not broil, grill, sauté or fry as well), but they have a firmer flesh and are more flavorful. They are good roasted, poached, or fricasseed. Economically, these are the best buys.

CAPONS: Roosters that have been castrated to improve the quality and flavor of the meat. They are only slightly older and larger than roasters but are considerably more tender, somewhat fattier, have a greater amount of meat on them, and are the most flavorful kind of chicken. They are fantastic for roasting and excellent for poaching. Capons are a good alternative to turkeys for holiday meals.

FOWL: The mature, adult members of the chicken world, about a year old and usually weighing from 4½ to 6 pounds. Fowl, though rich in flavor, are tough and stringy in texture and demand a moist cooking technique to tenderize the meat and extract the flavor. If not too old, fowl can be used for fricassees and stews. But as we have no way of knowing their age once they have been processed and plastic-wrapped, it's safer to use them for stocks and soups, where all the rich, gelatinous flavor is extracted and the meat fully tenderized. (Fowl are sometimes called "stewing hens," "old hens," "bro-hens," and "boiling hens." If there is any doubt in your mind as to whether or not you are buying a fowl, ask the butcher for an old bird that you can use for boiling and making soup.)

HOW DONE IS DONE?

After testing hundreds of chickens, I have decided that it is not the color of the juices that determines whether or not chicken is done but the internal temperature of the meat itself. The only accurate and dependable way of measuring this is to insert an instantly registering thermometer into the thickest part of the flesh, without touching the bone.

Chicken is done when the meat becomes opaque and the internal temperature reaches 165° F. for dark meat, 140° F. for white meat. In cases where a whole bird is being cooked, only the dark meat is tested. At these temperatures there is sometimes a slight rosiness to some of the juices, particularly if they have accumulated in the pocket around the thigh joint.

Some cookbook authors have said that you can test a chicken for doneness by pressing it with your finger and learning to feel how much resilience a properly cooked piece of chicken will have. It is the technique most often used by restaurant chefs, and it is the reason we rarely get a piece of properly cooked chicken in a restaurant.

A good deal more frequently one reads: "Pierce deeply with a fork or skewer. If the juices run clear, the chicken is done." I suspect the "Piercers" do a little better than the "Pushers" at guessing when their chicken is done, but they are merely guessing, and piercing presents special problems. When chicken is cooked in serving pieces, perhaps sautéed or fried, or even grilled or broiled, there simply are not enough juices in the chicken to run, no less to run in a definable color. On the other hand, when a whole chicken is cooked, a pocket of juices will form around the thigh joint, becoming the target for a piercer's fork or skewer. Unfortunately, by the time that pocket of juices has turned clear, the chicken is probably overcooked. And the juices will continue to run clear until the breast meat has dried out and begun to fall from the bones.

I've talked about the "Pushers" and the "Piercers," and now a few words about the "Jigglers." Occasionally one reads in a cookbook, "When the leg bone, or drumstick, moves easily in its socket, the chicken is done." This jiggling of the drumstick is not only an undependable way of testing for doneness but virtually impossible to execute if the chicken has been properly trussed, and rarely is a whole chicken cooked without trussing.

So don't worry about the color of the juices; just concern yourself with the flavor and texture of the meat.

"HOW MANY BREASTS DOES A CHICKEN HAVE?"

I remember a woman raising her hand during a cooking demonstration and asking, "How many breasts does a chicken have?" I was in the middle of burning a meringue and quipped back, "The same number as you do, madam." It was good for an audience laugh, which I needed at that moment, but unfortunately it completely passed over the question of what does constitute "a gastronomic breast." *Chickens have only one breast,* the entire area of the chest from the neck to the belly. This includes the skin, the delicate white meat or flesh, and the bones. A chicken breast is symmetrical; the right side of the breast is identical to the left side. Each half-breast has two fillets, a larger one with a smaller one attached to its underside.

A *suprême* is a boneless and skinless half-breast, and includes both the large and small fillets. Suprêmes are considered by all but dark-meat lovers to be the choicest morsel the chicken has to offer. The best way of obtaining suprêmes is still to buy whole fresh-killed chickens and either to bone, skin, and split the breasts yourself, or to ask your butcher to do it for you. Suprêmes can, of course, be purchased ready-prepared in almost any market that sells chicken in parts. But once the bones and skin have been removed, the breast begins to dehydrate and lose its tender juiciness and delicate flavor.

COLD CHICKEN

Cold chicken should not really be served cold but at room temperature. Once cooked, it is best to cool chicken to room temperature, cover it, and store it in the coolest part of the kitchen. Most chicken can be safely stored at room temperature for 24 hours.

For longer periods, of course, the chicken should be refrigerated. But refrigerating chicken dries it out and destroys much of its texture. Returning it to room temperature after it has been refrigerated will not restore the juicy, smooth texture to the now drier, coarser-textured meat.

REFRIGERATOR STORAGE

The heat-sealed, plastic-wrapped packages in which most supermarkets sell chicken are not satisfactory for home refrigeration. Remove the chicken from the package as soon as possible, cover with damp paper toweling, and then rewrap loosely in foil or plastic wrap. This will allow the chicken to breathe and at the same time prevent it from drying out. Giblet packages should be removed from the cavity and wrapped separately. In this way, chicken may safely be refrigerated for two to three days.

Wrapping paper: Chicken can be wrapped safely in plastic wrap; foil; waxed, silicone, or otherwise coated paper. Untreated paper often adheres to the chicken, causing refrigerator burns.

WASHING CHICKEN

Modern processing, storage, and transportation of chicken has virtually eliminated the need to wash a chicken.

The germs or bacteria in the chicken that can survive the cooking process are not at all disturbed by a bath, so a quick rinse under cold water or a light scrubbing with a damp cloth is of little value. If, as occasionally happens, the chicken has taken on a faint smell, rub it with a slice of lemon.

NOTES
ON FROZEN CHICKEN

Freezing chicken allows the careful shopper to save money by buying extra chicken on sale and to safely store it until needed. Freezing is also a way of saving odd bits and pieces of a chicken, like a neck or a pair of wing tips, until there is enough for stock or soup. Home freezing offers economy and convenience without too much loss of flavor and texture. The best chickens for home freezing weigh under 3 pounds; larger birds lose too much of their juiciness during freezing and thawing.

Frozen chicken must be thawed before cooking. The best way to thaw chicken is as slowly as possible. Simply transfer the freezer-wrapped chicken to the refrigerator and allow 24 to 36 hours to thaw. Once thawed, chicken should never be refrozen.

Freezing cooked chicken is generally not recommended; it destroys too much of the flavor and texture of the meat.

Freezer wrapping: When wrapping chicken for the freezer, be sure that the package is airtight. This prevents freezer burns. Plastic freezer bags with airtight seals, plastic containers with airtight lids, and coated freezer paper or plastic wrap make the best packagings. If using plastic wrap or freezer paper, however, be sure to double-wrap and tape securely. *Do not use aluminum foil.* It tends to crack, and also to tear other wrappings pushed against it.

Always label the packages with the date and contents. Frozen chicken can safely be stored in the freezer compartment of a refrigerator for 1 to 2 months, and 2 to 3 months in a deep freeze.

NUMBER
OF SERVINGS

Exactly how many people a recipe will serve, or the number of portions you can expect from a chicken of a certain weight, depends on how hungry everyone is, what else you are serving, and how you prepare it. A 3-pound chicken won't go very far as an *après*-ski meal for six hungry men, but when wrapped in brioche and served as part of a formal dinner, that same chicken will generously serve six.

As the chart below indicates, I plan ½ to ¾ pound of uncooked chicken per portion. I think it is better to have something

READY-TO-COOK WEIGHT	NUMBER OF SERVINGS
¾ to 1 pound (350–500 grams)	1
1½ to 2 pounds (750–1000 grams)	2 to 3
2½ to 3 pounds (1¼–1½ kilograms)	3 to 4
3½ to 4 pounds (1¾–2 kilograms)	4 to 6
4½ to 5 pounds (2¼–2½ kilograms)	6 to 8
5½ to 6 pounds (2¾–3 kilograms)	8 to 10

left over, rather than not have enough, because nothing, not even the bones of leftover chicken, goes to waste.

ORDERING CHICKEN
BY UNDRAWN WEIGHT

With the exception of certain Chinese markets and an ever-decreasing number of kosher butchers, commercially processed chickens in the United States are sold "ready-to-cook." But occasionally, especially if you live or travel abroad, it will be necessary to order chickens by undrawn or dressed weight, the weight of the bird before plucking and cleaning. A chicken in full plumage can look deceivingly large, and if you are unaccustomed to ordering by undrawn weight, you may feel cheated when you discover that you've lost a pound or two in having the bird drawn. The chart below compares ready-to-cook weight with the undrawn weight.

READY-TO-COOK WEIGHT	UNDRAWN WEIGHT
¾ to 1 pound (350–500 grams)	1¼ to 1½ pounds (500–700 grams)
1½ to 2 pounds (750–1000 grams)	2¼ to 2¾ pounds (1000–1250 grams)
2½ to 3 pounds (1¼–1½ kilograms)	3¼ to 3¾ pounds (1500–1750 grams)
3½ to 4 pounds (1¾–2 kilograms)	4¼ to 5 pounds (2–2½ kilograms)
4½ to 5 pounds (2¼–2½ kilograms)	5¾ to 6½ pounds (2¾–3¼ kilograms)
5½ to 6 pounds (2¾–3 kilograms)	7¼ to 8 pounds (3½–4 kilograms)

A WORD ABOUT METRIC

Metric measures are given in parentheses following each ingredient where different from standard American measures. Measuring cups and spoons, whether metric or standard, are interchangeable. A standard tablespoon, for example, has a capacity of ½ fluid ounce, or 14.7 milliliters. A metric tablespoon is 15 milliliters.

Unfortunately, the metrification board has decreed that we shall measure liquids in milliliters. There is a system using deciliters which most of the world uses, and which I think is better. Anyway, a metric cup will be 250 milliliters. The metric cup will be divided into half cups, third cups, and quarter cups. A quarter cup, then, is 62.5 milliliters. Since I think it unreasonable to expect anyone to think in quantities like 62.5 milliliters, I have kept the measures in this book in cups. Liquid measuring cups will, I hope, give milliliters on one side and metric cups divided into thirds and quarters on the other side.

Even though we will be purchasing in grams and kilograms, the word "pound" will probably remain part of our vocabulary. A metric pound is 500 grams, or ½ kilogram. Where can sizes have been specified, I have chosen the nearest equivalent size from the list of metric sizes suggested by the Bureau of Standards.

CHICKEN AND WINE

Chicken is one of the world's most versatile foods. Depending on the recipe, virtually any wine produced can be served appropriately with chicken. The wine can be from the lightest and driest to the most lusciously sweet of whites, or from the fruitiest to the richest, most full-bodied of reds. Your choice of wine should depend entirely on the strength of the flavors and textures in the recipe. Wine and food flavors are best when they complement each other. There should be a balance between them which creates a harmony—neither the flavor of the food nor the flavor of the wine overpowering the other.

Chicken dishes range from delicate and subtle to big, hearty, and robust, with an enormous range of flavors and textures in between. Wines, too, are available in a full spectrum of aroma, flavor, and depth. When selecting a wine to accompany a particular dish, choose one that is similar in character to the combination of flavors in the recipe. For example, poached chicken with no sauce, or with a very simple white sauce, might be enhanced by a light, delicate wine that will not mask the chicken's soft, natural flavors. A young, very dry white Chardonnay from California or Burgundy would be a perfect match because of its lightness and delicacy. Whereas chicken Kiev, with the added richness and texture of butter and bread crumbs, would require a bigger and more complex wine such as one of the great white Burgundies in the Montrachet family, or a fine château-bottled red wine from Bordeaux's Médoc region. A gutsy, garlicky chicken cacciatore, on the other hand, demands a robust red that can stand up to the aroma and flavor of the garlic, the acidity of the tomatoes, and the coarseness of the textures in this hunter's dish. Thus, a Barolo or a Chianti *classico* or a Côtes du Rhône would all be good choices. All are full-bodied red wines, able to hold their own against the cacciatore.

Most of the recipes in this book are accompanied by two wine recommendations, some by as many as three or four. The recommendations are specific regarding the type of wine and its region of origin. Sometimes these suggestions include both a white wine and a red. Again, this is because the flavor and body of a wine are far more important than its color. Ultimately, though, the most important consideration in selecting a wine is to find one that suits your palate and your pocketbook.

1

ROASTING

PREHISTORIC MAN created roasting, or more accurately spit-roasting, when he first suspended a piece of meat with a green stick through it over a fire and rested the stick on stones at either end of the fire. Spit-roasting survived virtually unchanged from 500,000 B.C. until the middle of the nineteenth century. But let's look for a moment at what an eighteenth-century woman had to do to roast a chicken.

First she had to find a good, plump chicken of the size she wanted. Next the bird had to be killed, plucked, and drawn—a chore the eighteenth-century housewife accepted more graciously than we would today. Then she had to check the spit. If the spit had been well scrubbed with sand and water the last time she roasted, and carefully dried and stored, it would be ready to use. But if it had rusted, or had been coated in a layer of melted fat to prevent rusting, water would have to be boiled and the spit cleaned. One of the eighteenth century's more important English cookbook authors was Hannah Glasse, and to her, good roasting meant a good fire. She advised the housewife to lay "a pretty little brisk fire" so that the chicken would "be done quick and nice." A chicken roasted slowly, she writes, "would not eat near so sweet, or look so beautiful to the eye." The chicken would be roasted in front of the fire in a tin or copper Dutch oven, designed very much like the rotisserie of today—but the cook had to do the turning. It took a great deal of practice and experience to learn to lay the fire properly, to control the heat it generated by moving the oven slightly forward or slightly back, and when and how to poke and spread the ash-laden coals to generate just the right amount of heat over just the right area.

To me, the recommended cooking times are by far the most fascinating aspect of eighteenth-century recipes for roast chicken. Small chickens were to be roasted for 20 to 30 minutes, larger ones for 1 hour to 1 hour and 15 minutes. As those cooking times are almost identical to the cooking times recommended in this book, it means that the heat radiated into those often flimsy tin ovens was between 450° F. and 500° F. And that means that the roast chicken of the eighteenth century was juicier and better tasting than most roast chicken today.

For the housewife, roasting chicken changed little until the time of Alexis Soyer in the mid-nineteenth century. Soyer was a creative genius, and a man of great humanitarian spirit. He invented the first compact modern stove and a small-sized oven for the working-class family. It even had a controllable heat source using gas, then the latest form of fuel for cooking. Soyer, the father of modern cooking, would feel a sense of awe in today's kitchen. A self-cleaning push-button oven with thermostatically controlled heat and a built-in electric rotisserie! a refrigerator! a food processor! Soyer's compact modern oven was the first significant change—indeed, it was a revolution—to occur in roasting for half a million years. Chickens left the spit and the blazing fire of the hearth to sit peacefully on a roasting pan in the darkness of a warm, modern oven.

Put most simply, the four essentials of roasting are (1) trussing, (2) sealing, (3) turning, and (4) using a rack. Trussing is simply a way of tying the chicken so it holds its shape during cooking. It makes the chicken easier to handle and to carve, and it makes the final presentation of the chicken attractive.

Critical to good roasting is forming a seal on the outside of the chicken to hold in its natural moisture and juices. When the chicken comes into contact with heat, a series of chemical reactions occur which eventually cause the natural sugars in the chicken to caramelize, turning the skin brown and sealing the meat. In order to caramelize quickly and evenly, the skin must be moisture-free. This is why the recipe reads "Pat the chicken dry." Drying the skin prepares the bird for rubbing with some sort of fat, usually butter or oil, and for basting. The fat acts as a screen, or one-way mirror. It allows the heat to pass into the chicken, but forms a barrier which prevents the moisture in the chicken—which has turned to steam—from escaping. If the chicken is properly basted during roasting, the protective shield will hold, and consequently the chicken will remain juicier.

The third principle of roasting is turning. In the master recipe for roast chicken, the chicken is roasted for one third of the cooking time on each side of its breast, and for the final third on its back. Turning the chicken guarantees even cooking and coloring, and prevents the juices of the delicate breast meat from draining down into a pocket around the legs and thighs.

Roasting is cooking by dry heat. To ensure that there is dry heat circulating completely around the chicken, a rack is placed under the bird. If the chicken is cooked in an open pan without a rack, the bottom of the chicken stews in its own juices while the top is roasting.

There is nothing very difficult about roasting. Once you have roasted a simple, unstuffed chicken, the rest of the chapter will be easy to understand—for it is little more than a series of variations on the master recipe. Following the recipe for roast chicken is a section on flavored butters and oils, and a section on stuffings.

The second master recipe is for a split roast chicken, stuffed or unstuffed. Here the variation is in the butchering. Rather than the chicken being roasted whole, it is split down the back. With the chicken in this shape, no trussing is needed, nor is it necessary to turn the chicken while roasting, but you should baste it and use a rack. The final master recipe is for spit-roasted chicken. The chicken is trussed in the normal way, but there is no need to use a rack or turn the chicken by hand. The spit, which keeps the chicken suspended in the middle of the oven, ensures an even circulation of heat around the bird and turns the chicken at the same time. Instead of brushing the chicken with melted butter or oil as in the previous recipes, seal the chicken by tying strips of bacon around it. As the chicken turns on the spit, it bastes itself in the dripping bacon fat.

Roasting is the oldest, simplest, and even today the most popular way of cooking chicken. Whether lavishly smothered in rich, sweet butter, or split and gently perfumed with ginger oil, what could be better for a family meal or that special dinner party than the lovely textures and flavor of a juicy roast chicken?

ROAST CHICKEN

❖❖❖

MASTER RECIPE

❖

You can be taught to cook, but
must be born knowing how to roast.

FRENCH PROVERB

The *perfectly* roasted chicken, with its crisp, buttery, golden-brown skin and moist, tender flesh, rarely reaches our table. It doesn't take a great cook to produce a beautifully roasted bird, but it does require a little patience and care. Overcooking and underattention are the greatest faults of the cook who thinks a chicken can be thrown into the oven and will all but cook itself. It won't! You need to hover around the oven, turning the bird and keeping it well basted, and showing it you care.

1 2½- to 3-pound chicken, at
   room temperature (1¼–
   1½ kilograms)
8 Tablespoons butter,
   semisoft but still cold (re-

move from the refrigerator
1 hour before needed), or
⅓ cup oil
Salt
Freshly ground black pepper

This recipe is for a 2½- to 3-pound chicken. For chickens of other weights, consult the roasting chart on page 9 for the exact cooking time.

See pages 10 to 18 for flavored butters and oils.*

Preheat oven to 450° F.

---

* For the calorie-conscious, roast the chicken using an inexpensive oil and serve the juices that accumulate in the cavity and on the serving board as the sauce. Unfortunately, because of its high calorie count, the calorie-counter should not eat the skin.

Remove any excess fat from the vent of the chicken. Season the inside of the chicken with salt and pepper. Place about 2 tablespoons of butter in the cavity, or rub lightly with oil. Pat the outside of the chicken thoroughly dry to ensure proper browning. Truss the chicken (see page 221).

Rub the chicken generously on all sides with about half the remaining butter or oil. Sprinkle with salt and pepper, massaging the salt and pepper into the butter.

Place the chicken on one side of its breast on a rack in a shallow roasting pan. Using a rack allows for even heat circulation around the bird, and placing the chicken on its side prevents the juices from draining down and out of the breast.

Place the roasting pan on a shelf in the lower third of a pre-heated oven. This means the chicken itself is in the middle of the oven.

Melt the remaining butter.

After one third of the cooking time, 15 minutes in this case, turn the chicken onto the other side of its breast, and baste generously with the remaining butter or oil. I find that basting with a pastry brush is faster and easier than with a spoon or bulb baster. Basting should be done as quickly as possible to prevent a loss of oven heat and to prevent the chicken from cooling. Continue roasting the chicken for the second third of the estimated cooking time, or another 15 minutes.

By now the chicken will be well into its browning process, and the fat will be sputtering in the pan.

For the final third of its cooking time, turn the chicken onto its back, and baste lavishly with the juices from the roasting pan.

TEST THE CHICKEN FOR DONENESS: After 45 minutes of roasting time, the low end of the estimated cooking time on the roasting chart (page 9), insert an instantly registering thermometer into the thickest part of the thigh without touching the bone. The chicken is perfectly cooked when the internal temperature of the thigh reaches 165° F. If necessary, return to the oven for another 5 minutes, and test again.

When done, transfer to a warm platter or carving board and remove the trussing string. Drain the juices from the cavity and either mix with the pan drippings, or use to flavor the gravy or sauce. Allow the chicken to rest at room temperature for 10 to 15 minutes before carving. This gives the juices a chance to settle into the flesh rather than gush out onto the platter when the chicken is carved. For carving directions, see page 239.

SAUCE: The rich, buttery pan drippings provide all the sauce needed. Spoon a tablespoon or so over each serving.

VEGETABLE AND WINE NOTES: A simple roast chicken almost screams for potatoes: sautéed, fried, scalloped, or perhaps pommes Anna, and a buttered green vegetable—peas, beans, broccoli, or spinach.

A great many wines can comfortably grace the table with a roast chicken. Your choice, which could be red or white, will depend on such things as personal preference, the time of day, and your guests. Generally, though, the most palate-pleasing would be a medium-priced red Bordeaux or a California Cabernet Sauvignon. If you prefer a white, choose a Chardonnay from California or a Mâcon Blanc from Burgundy.

For a truly sumptuous dinner, a classed, and therefore more expensive, red growth from Bordeaux's Médoc or Graves areas would be lovely. When serving roast chicken for lunch, a light red wine such as Bardolino or even a medium-dry white wine, such as Sauvignon Blanc, would be nice.

There are probably more variations possible with a roast chicken than with any other recipe in this book. But there is one variation I adamantly oppose: *Do not lower the cooking temperature!* Unrivaled for roasting chicken is 450° F. It seals in all of the juices and completes the roasting before the meat has a chance to dry out. None of the lower temperatures comes even close!

There is one small disadvantage to roasting chicken at this high a heat. The natural juices of the chicken, when heated this rapidly, turn to steam. As basting has sealed the skin and prevented the steam from escaping, it stretches and puffs the skin instead. Served hot, this is no problem. But when the chicken cools, the stretched skin becomes limp and wrinkled. All in all, it seems a small disadvantage for so juicy and delicious a way of roasting chicken.

The French often stuff a few sprigs of tarragon into the cavity of the chicken before roasting. And while the combination of sweet, fresh tarragon and chicken in one of the best, a few sprigs of almost any fresh herb can be used—or half a lemon, a piece of onion, a few garlic cloves, a shallot or two, or a couple of celery ribs.

If you prefer to make a sauce instead of just using the pan drippings as recommended in the recipe, while the chicken is resting, skim the fat from the pan and deglaze it with white wine, Cognac, or stock. Add a bit more stock or water, and either reduce it to form a sauce or thicken in with a few bits of *beurre manié*. Add a few sautéed mushrooms and a little Madeira and cream for a mushroom gravy, or cooked and chopped giblets for a giblet gravy, or prepare a rich onion gravy by stirring in some cracklings (see page 181); or add cream and stock for a cream gravy, and perhaps thicken it with egg yolks instead of the kneaded butter and flour of a *beurre manié*.

ROASTING CHART
(Unstuffed Whole Roast Chicken)

READY-TO-COOK WEIGHT	OVEN TEMP.	APPROXIMATE COOKING TIME (IN MINUTES)
¾ to 1 pound (350–500 grams)	450° F.	25 to 30 25 to 30
1½ to 2 pounds (750–1000 grams)	450° F.	35 to 40 40 to 45
2½ to 3 pounds (1¼–1½ kilograms)	450° F.	45 to 50 45 to 55
3½ to 4 pounds (1¾–2 kilograms)	450° F.	50 to 60 55 to 65
4½ to 5 pounds (2¼–2½ kilograms)	450° F.	55 to 65 65 to 75
5½ to 6 pounds (2¾–3 kilograms)	450° F.	65 to 75 75 to 85

You can also serve roast chicken with many of the sauces recommended in Chapter 9.

The liver, or liver and gizzard, can be cooked in the pan while the chicken is roasting, and then quietly eaten by the cook.

FLAVORED BUTTERS

———— ❖❖❖ ————

Flavored butters are a simple and easy way to add variety and excitement to a roast chicken. Almost any herb and many spices will flatter the flavor of a roast chicken, as well as garlic, shallots, mustard, Tabasco sauce, red or white wine, and Cognac, to mention only a few. You might also try rubbing some under the skin as directed in Marion Cunningham's recipe on page 123.

When making a good herb butter, be sure to start with cold butter, which becomes light and fluffy when beaten and makes an excellent base for the addition of herbs and flavorings. Soft butter, on the other hand, becomes slick and greasy and makes it difficult to distribute the herbs evenly. And it is not easy to beat liquids—like lemon juice, which balances the flavor of the chives in the master recipe—into butter unless there is something already in the butter to absorb them. So the temperature and the sequence are important in making a good herb butter.

There are a great many uses for herb butters besides just spreading them on roast chicken. They can be used to enrich and flavor sauces and to enliven the taste of simple green vegetables. Also, a pat can be placed on top of any kind of broiled or grilled meat or fish. They are also good on baked potatoes, and you can even stir a few tablespoons into scrambled eggs. Why not make a double or triple batch and store it in the freezer?

CHIVE BUTTER

MASTER RECIPE

Fresh chives offer a beautiful, soft onion flavor to roast chicken. I am especially fond of rubbing this chive butter under the skin of the bird, and using plain butter on the outside of the chicken.

8 Tablespoons cold butter
½ cup chopped fresh chives
¼ teaspoon salt: omit *if using salted butter*
½ teaspoon freshly ground black pepper
1½ teaspoons lemon juice

Beat the butter until light and fluffy and slightly pale in color. This can be done with an electric beater or in an electric mixer, or by mashing the butter against the side of a bowl with the back of a wooden spoon and then beating furiously.

Add the chives, salt if used, and pepper, and mix thoroughly. Add the lemon juice, beating slowly at first to avoid splashing, and then more vigorously as it starts to become absorbed.

Refrigerate for 15 to 20 minutes before using, so that the butter can become firm enough to spread easily onto the chicken. Butters made in advance and stored in the refrigerator will return to a readily spreadable consistency after 45 minutes to an hour at room temperature. Herb butter can be frozen safely in a tightly covered container for several months.

Makes enough for 1 large or 2 small chickens.

MIXED HERB BUTTER

— ❖❖❖ —

This is a good butter to have on hand—not only for roasting chicken, but for a multitude of other uses. It makes an excellent snail butter; it can be used to top a broiled or grilled steak or piece of fish; and it is delicious tossed with boiled potatoes or steamed peas, broccoli, or green beans.

8 *Tablespoons cold butter*
2 *Tablespoons chopped fresh parsley*
2 *Tablespoons chopped fresh chives*
2 *Tablespoons chopped fresh tarragon, or 1 teaspoon crushed dried tarragon*

1 *Tablespoon finely chopped shallots*
1 *garlic clove, finely chopped*
¼ *teaspoon salt:* omit *if using salted butter*
¼ *teaspoon freshly ground black pepper*

Beat the butter until light and fluffy. Add the remaining ingredients, and mix well. Refrigerate for 15 to 20 minutes before using.

Makes enough for 1 large or 2 small chickens.

PARSLEY BUTTER

— ❖❖❖ —

8 *Tablespoons cold butter*
½ *cup chopped parsley*
¼ *teaspoon salt:* omit *if using salted butter*

¼ *teaspoon freshly ground black pepper*

Beat the butter until light and fluffy. Add the parsley, salt if used, and pepper, and mix well. Refrigerate for 15 to 20 minutes before using.

Makes enough for 1 large or 2 small chickens.

VARIATIONS

LEMON PARSLEY BUTTER: Add 2 teaspoons lemon juice and the grated zest of half a lemon. Beat slowly to prevent splashing.

TARRAGON BUTTER: Substitute tarragon for the parsley, and add 1 tablespoon chopped shallots and 1 garlic clove, finely chopped.

ROSEMARY BUTTER: Substitute 2 to 3 tablespoons of chopped fresh rosemary, or 1½ teaspoons crushed dried rosemary, for the parsley; add the grated zest of half a lemon, and a little extra freshly ground black pepper.

GINGER BUTTER

——— ❖❖❖ ———

This butter gives the chicken a warm and inviting ginger perfume. The cinnamon and garlic help to round off the flavor, as does the soy sauce used in place of salt.

8 *Tablespoons cold, unsalted*
  butter
1 *Tablespoon ground ginger*
¼ *teaspoon ground cinnamon*
1 *garlic clove, finely*
  chopped

1 *teaspoon freshly ground*
  black pepper
1 *teaspoon soy sauce*

Beat the butter until light and fluffy. Add the ginger, cinnamon, garlic, and pepper, and mix well. Add the soy sauce, beating slowly at first to prevent splashing. Refrigerate for 15 to 20 minutes before using.

Makes enough for 1 large or 2 small chickens.

CHILI BUTTER

———— ❖❖❖ ————

Not only will this chili butter flavor the skin of a roast chicken and act as a protective screen to keep the chicken moist, but it will also serve as an excellent browning aid.

8 *Tablespoons cold butter*
1 *Tablespoon chili powder*
¼ *teaspoon crushed dried oregano*
¼ *teaspoon paprika*
¼ *teaspoon Tabasco sauce or cayenne, optional*

1 *teaspoon tomato paste*
¼ *teaspoon salt:* omit *if using salted butter*
¼ *teaspoon freshly ground black pepper*

Beat the butter until light and fluffy. Add the remaining ingredients, and mix well. Refrigerate for 15 to 20 minutes before using.

Makes enough for 1 large or 2 small chickens.

CURRY BUTTER

———— ❖❖❖ ————

Premixed curry powders are far more a Western convenience than a reflection of our understanding of Indian cooking. Most jars and tins of curry powder are old and stale, having lost most of their flavor and fragrance long before we purchased them. The best curry powders available are often labeled "Madras curry powder" and are usually manufactured by companies whose names are unfamiliar. Look around the specialty food shops for one of those; I think you'll be surprised at how much difference a full, fragrant curry powder can make.

8 *Tablespoons cold butter*
2 *to 3 teaspoons Madras curry*
  powder
1 *garlic clove, finely chopped*
¼ *teaspoon salt:* omit *if using*
  salted butter

½ *teaspoon freshly ground*
  black pepper
1 *teaspoon lemon juice*

Beat the butter until light and fluffy. Add the curry powder, garlic, salt if used, and pepper, and mix well. Add the lemon juice, beating slowly at first to prevent splashing. Refrigerate for 15 to 20 minutes before using.

Makes enough for 1 large or 2 small chickens.

GARLIC BUTTER

One of my great frustrations is to hear someone tell me they have flavored a recipe with "a hint of garlic." And one of my greatest joys is to hear someone tell me they are growing elephant garlic in their yard. Elephant garlic is a variety of garlic whose bulbs grow to almost the size of a medium onion and which has a sweeter, less harsh taste. About 3 or 4 of those cloves would be fantastic in this butter.

8 *Tablespoons cold butter*
3 *to 4 garlic cloves, finely*
  chopped
¼ *teaspoon salt:* omit *if using*
  salted butter

¼ *teaspoon freshly ground*
  black pepper

Beat the butter until light and fluffy. Add the garlic, salt if used, and pepper, and mix well. Refrigerate for 15 to 20 minutes before using.

Makes enough for 1 large or 2 small chickens.

GREEN PEPPERCORN BUTTER

❖❖❖

Green peppercorns are not new spice, but rather the very young form of one that has been with us for centuries. They are the unripened berries that later in life could be dried to make black peppercorns, or dried and skinned to make white peppercorns. They are available packed in water or brine, or dehydrated. The dried ones I have tasted were not very exciting, so look for ones packed in water or brine. Green peppercorns are also fantastic with fish, and they seem to burst with excitement when added to white sauces. A hint of cinnamon with them is heavenly!

8 Tablespoons cold butter
2 to 3 Tablespoons green
  peppercorns
1 garlic clove
⅛ teaspoon cinnamon

¼ teaspoon salt: omit *if using*
  salted butter
¼ teaspoon freshly ground
  black pepper

Beat the butter until light and fluffy. Using a mortar and pestle, mash the peppercorns and garlic to a paste, or smash with the side of a cook's knife and chop very finely. Mix with the cinnamon, salt if used, and pepper. Combine with the butter, and mix well. Refrigerate for 15 to 20 minutes before using.
Makes enough for 1 large or 2 small chickens.

FLAVORED OILS

❖❖❖

Oils can be flavored in much the same way as butter, using herbs, spices, and other seasonings and flavorings. Substitute oil for the butter in any of the flavored butter recipes, create your own, or try the ones suggested below.

BASIC HERBED OIL

———— ❖❖❖ ————

Use whatever herb or combination of herbs you have available. For some specific ideas, peruse the section of herbed butters. If you grow your own herbs, you might have lemon thyme on hand, and this is where you use it—with a clove of garlic and some salt and pepper. Be creative—more often than not it will be delicious.

½ *cup oil*
¼ *cup chopped fresh herbs,*
   or 1 to 2 Tablespoons
   crushed, dried herbs
1 *to 2 Tablespoons chopped*
   shallots (optional)

1 *to 2 garlic cloves, finely*
   chopped (optional)
½ *teaspoon salt*
¼ *teaspoon freshly ground*
   black pepper

Combine all ingredients, and mix well. When using fresh herbs, or shallots or garlic as additional flavorings, do not keep the oil for more than a day or two, as it may sour.

Makes enough for 1 large or 2 small chickens.

PAPRIKA OIL

———— ❖❖❖ ————

A bright red, first-quality Hungarian paprika, with its aromatic spiciness and sweet, smoky flavor, adds a fragrant flavor to chicken, in addition to acting as an excellent browning aid. If you use paprika, it is well worth your time to find a superior product. Most of the commercial paprikas found in supermarkets, which seem to get sprinkled on everything from cottage cheese to broiled fish, are little more than tasteless, burnt-orange coloring agents.

½ *cup oil*
2 *teaspoons paprika, prefer-*
  ably first-quality Hungarian
1 *teaspoon lemon juice*

½ *teaspoon salt*
¼ *teaspoon freshly ground*
  black pepper

Combine all ingredients, and mix well.
Makes enough for 1 large or 2 small chickens.

OIL WITH TURMERIC, GARLIC, AND BLACK PEPPER

❖❖❖

½ *cup oil*
2 *Tablespoons ground*
  turmeric
2 *to* 3 *garlic cloves, finely*
  chopped

½ *teaspoon salt*
2 *teaspoons coarsely ground*
  black pepper

Combine all ingredients, and mix well.
Makes enough for 1 large or 2 small chickens.

MUSTARD-FLAVORED OIL

❖❖❖

2 *Tablespoons French mus-*
  tard, preferably a Dijon or
  Meaux mustard
½ *cup oil*

¼ *teaspoon salt*
½ *teaspoon freshly ground*
  black pepper

Combine all ingredients, and mix well. Mustard and oil are
sometimes difficult to combine, and I find that shaking them in a
small, tightly covered jar or container is best.
Makes enough for 1 large or 2 small chickens.

ROAST STUFFED CHICKEN

❖❖❖

Stuffings are a good way to add flavor and variation to what might otherwise be just another roast chicken. In addition, they provide a relatively inexpensive way to stretch the meal. There are two ways to stuff a chicken. The traditional method is simply to fill the cavity of a whole chicken. The other, less popular, though in many respects a far more exciting method, is to split the chicken and stuff it under the skin. Any of the stuffings in this chapter can be used with either method, and there is a master recipe for each.

Do not overstuff. The chicken should never be packed with stuffiing, but only loosely filled. As the chicken cooks, the stuffing will absorb moisture from the bird and expand slightly, so leave enough room to allow for this. Also, unless the skin over the vent has been badly torn during the evisceration or the stuffing, there is no need to sew it up. By trussing the chicken according to the directions on page 221, the vent will be sufficiently closed to hold the stuffing in and to allow the steam which builds up in the chicken to escape without causing the stuffing to explode out unattractively at both ends.

ROAST STUFFED CHICKEN
(WHOLE)

❖❖❖

MASTER RECIPE

❖

1 4½- to 5-pound chicken, at
    room temperature (2–2¼
    kilograms)
Stuffing, from any of the
    stuffing recipes on pages
    22 to 30, or a favorite
    stuffing of your choice

8 Tablespoons butter, semi-
    soft but still cold (remove
    from the refrigerator 1
    hour before needed), or
    ⅓ cup oil
Salt
Freshly ground black pepper

*This recipe is for a 4½- to 5-pound chicken. For chickens of
other weights, consult the roasting chart on page 21 for the
exact cooking time. If roasting 2 small—say, 2- to 2½-pound—
chickens, add 10 minutes to the approximate cooking time.*

Preheat oven to 450° F.

If the stuffing has been made in advance, bring it back to room
temperature before filling the chicken. Stand the chicken on its
neck end, remove any excess fat from the vent, and *loosely*
spoon the stuffing into the cavity. Extra stuffing can be baked
separately.

Pat the chicken thoroughly dry to ensure proper browning,
being certain to remove any bits of stuffing that may be stuck to
the outside of the chicken. Truss the chicken (see page 221).

Rub the chicken generously on all sides with about half the
butter or oil. Sprinkle with salt and pepper, massaging the salt
and pepper into the butter or oil.

Place the chicken on one side of its breast on a rack in a
shallow roasting pan. Using a rack allows for even heat circulation around the bird, and placing the chicken on its side prevents
the juices from draining down and out of the breast.

Place the roasting pan on a shelf in the lower third of a preheated oven. This means that the chicken itself is in the middle of the oven.

Melt the remaining butter.

After one third of the cooking time, 25 minutes in this case, turn the chicken onto the other side of its breast, and baste generously with the remaining butter or oil. Continue roasting the chicken for the second third of the estimated cooking time, in this case another 25 minutes.

For the final third of its cooking time, turn the chicken onto its back, and baste lavishly with the juices from the pan.

TEST THE CHICKEN FOR DONENESS: After 70 minutes of roasting time, the low end of the estimated cooking time on the roasting chart, check for doneness (see page 7).

ROASTING CHART
(Whole Stuffed Chicken)

READY-TO-COOK WEIGHT	OVEN TEMP.	APPROXIMATE COOKING TIME (IN MINUTES)
¾ to 1 pound (350–500 grams)	450° F.	30 to 35 / 30 to 35
1½ to 2 pounds (750–1000 grams)	450° F.	40 to 50 / 45 to 55
2½ to 3 pounds (1¼–1½ kilograms)	450° F.	55 to 60 / 60 to 70
3½ to 4 pounds (1¾–2 kilograms)	450° F.	65 to 75 / 75 to 85
4½ to 5 pounds (2¼–2½ kilograms)	450° F.	70 to 80 / 80 to 90
5½ to 6 pounds (2¾–3 kilograms)	450° F.	75 to 85 / 90 to 100

When done, transfer to a warm platter or carving board. Remove the trussing string and allow the chicken to rest at room temperature for 5 to 10 minutes before carving so that the juices can settle into the flesh. For carving directions, see page 239.

SAUCE: The rich, buttery pan drippings provide all the sauce needed. Spoon a tablespoon or so over each serving. If you prefer a sauce to the pan drippings recommended in this recipe, refer to the notes on page 9.

Choose the vegetables and wine in relation to the flavor of the stuffing.

SIMPLE GRAPE STUFFING

—————— ❖❖❖ ——————

This is probably the simplest stuffing ever. Use a large bunch of sweet, seedless green grapes. Remove the stems, peel them only if you are patient and a perfectionist—I'm not—and fill the cavity of the chicken with a few handfuls of the grapes. As the chicken roasts, something wonderful happens to the grapes. They absorb the juices from the chicken and become mellow and sweet, rich and round in flavor, and are sensually very exciting to eat.

Serve with crisp potatoes, a fresh green vegetable like broccoli, and either a medium-dry white wine such as a Vouvray from the Loire Valley or a Riesling from Alsace, both in France, or experiment with a sparkling Asti Spumante from Italy's Piedmont. There is practically no other entrée for which I would recommend Asti Spumante because of its grapey bouquet and sweet taste, but its marriage with a grape-stuffed chicken is utterly exquisite.

LEMON PARSLEY STUFFING

❖❖❖

The flavor of this stuffing is so simple, so honest, and so delicious that there never seems to be enough of it. It has a clean, refreshing taste and a lightness that is uncommon in stuffings. It's also fabulous for a Thanksgiving turkey.

6 *Tablespoons butter*	3 *eggs, well beaten*
1 *medium onion, chopped*	¾ *cup melted butter*
3 *cups fresh bread crumbs*	*Salt*
Grated zest of 3 lemons	*Freshly ground black pepper*
1½ *cups chopped parsley*	

Melt the 6 tablespoons of butter in a skillet over medium-low heat. When hot, add the onions and sauté until tender and translucent, about 4 minutes.

In a large mixing bowl, combine the bread crumbs, lemon zest, parsley, and sautéed onions. Stir in the beaten eggs and melted butter, and mix well. Season with salt and pepper to taste.

Serve with boiled potatoes, a simple green vegetable, and with either a fragrant, not-too-dry white wine such as a California Chénin Blanc or, if you prefer, a fruity red wine such as Beaujolais from France, a Gamay Beaujolais from California, or a Valpolicella from Italy's Veronese area.

Makes enough for 1 large or 2 small chickens.

OYSTER STUFFING

———— ❖❖❖ ————

They say oysters are a cruel
meat, because we eat them alive;
then they are an uncharitable meat for
we leave nothing to the poor;
and they are an ungodly meat
because we never say grace.

JONATHAN SWIFT

4 *Tablespoons butter*
½ *medium onion, finely*
 chopped
1 *shallot, finely chopped*
1 *leek, white part only, finely*
 chopped
1 *garlic clove, finely*
 chopped
1 *celery rib, finely chopped*
½ *green pepper, finely*
 chopped
2 *cups fresh bread crumbs*

18 *oysters, shucked, drained,*
 and coarsely chopped
½ *cup chopped watercress*
 leaves or spinach leaves
1 *Tablespoon lemon juice*
½ *teaspoon thyme*
1 *teaspoon grated nutmeg*
2 *eggs, well beaten*
¼ *cup melted butter*
Salt
Freshly ground black pepper

Melt the 4 tablespoons of butter in a skillet over medium-low heat. When hot, add the onion, shallot, leek, garlic, celery, and green pepper. Sauté until tender and translucent, about 6 minutes.

In a mixing bowl, combine the sautéed vegetables with the bread crumbs, oysters, watercress, lemon juice, thyme, nutmeg, eggs, and melted butter. Mix well, and season to taste with salt and pepper.

Serve with broccoli or spinach and a bone-dry, crisp white wine such as Chablis from France or Orvieto Secco from Italy.

Makes enough for 1 large or 2 small chickens.

CELERY AND HAM STUFFING

❖❖❖

This stuffing should be made with good, crisp celery, rich in color and with the leaves still on the top if at all possible. The ham adds a nice color contrast to the celery, with the onion, garlic, lemon, and seasonings pulling the tastes together and rounding them off. It should be slightly drier than most stuffings; the suet will moisten it during the roasting. Use it as a basic stuffing, a replacement for the boringly traditional onion and sage stuffing.

4 *Tablespoons butter*
2 *to 3 celery ribs, chopped*
½ *small onion, finely chopped*
1 *garlic clove, finely chopped*
Grated zest of ½ lemon
¼ *cup chopped parsley*
½ *teaspoon crushed dried thyme*
⅛ *teaspoon crushed dried sage leaves,* not *ground or powdered sage*

¼ *teaspoon crushed dried marjoram*
½ *cup diced ham, about 2 to 3 ounces (50–75 grams)*
1 *cup fresh bread crumbs*
2 *Tablespoons chicken stock*
⅓ *cup shredded suet*
Salt
Freshly ground black pepper

Melt the butter in a skillet over medium-low heat. When hot, add the celery, onion, and garlic, and sauté until tender and translucent, about 6 minutes. The celery should be tender but still have a slight crunchiness. Add the lemon zest, parsley, thyme, sage, marjoram, and ham. Sauté for 1 minute longer.

In a mixing bowl, combine the bread crumbs, suet, sautéed vegetables, and ham. Add the stock, and mix well. Season with salt and pepper to taste.

Serve with potatoes, carrots, or zucchini, and a medium-bodied red wine such as a Bardolino from Italy's northern Lake Garda-Verona region, or a Beaujolais from France.

Makes enough for 1 large or 2 small chickens.

WHOLE-WHEAT
AND SAUSAGE STUFFING

——————— ❖❖❖ ———————

This is an interesting stuffing in that it uses as a base whole-wheat bread crumbs, which have an almost nutty flavor that is particularly flattering to the sausage.

4 *Tablespoons butter or oil*
1 *medium onion, finely chopped*
1 *celery rib, finely chopped*
1 *garlic clove, finely chopped*
½ *pound breakfast sausage meat, crumbled* (200–250 grams)
¼ *teaspoon crushed dried marjoram*

½ *teaspoon crushed dried thyme*
2 *cups fresh whole-wheat bread crumbs*
1 *egg, well beaten*
⅓ *cup chicken stock*
Salt
Freshly ground black pepper

Melt the butter or oil in a large skillet over medium heat. When hot, add the onion, celery, and garlic, and sauté for 2 to 3 minutes. Add the sausage meat, marjoram, and thyme, and sauté for another 2 to 3 minutes until all the raw color of the sausage meat has disappeared.

In a large bowl, combine the bread crumbs with the vegetables and sausage. Mix well. Stir in the beaten egg and stock. Season with salt and pepper to taste.

Serve with glazed carrots or turnips, green beans, and a hearty, robust red wine such as Chianti *classico* from Italy, Corbières from the south of France, or a Pinot Noir from California.

Makes enough for 1 large or 2 small chickens.

OLIVE STUFFING

————— ❖❖❖ —————

. . . for olive lovers only!

4 *Tablespoons butter*
1 *medium onion, finely chopped*
1 *garlic clove, finely chopped*
3 *cups fresh bread crumbs*
¼ *cup chicken stock*

2 *eggs, well beaten*
1 *cup black olives, pitted and coarsely chopped*
Salt
Freshly ground black pepper

Melt the butter in a skillet over medium-low heat. When hot, add the onions and garlic, and sauté until tender and translucent, about 4 minutes.

Place the bread crumbs in a mixing bowl and moisten with the stock and beaten eggs. Add the olives and sautéed onions. Mix well. Season with salt and pepper to taste.

Serve with a buttered green vegetable and baked tomatoes, and a full-bodied, almost pungent red wine such as a Barbera from California or from Italy.

Makes enough for 1 large or 2 small chickens.

RICOTTA STUFFING

————— ❖❖❖ —————

Ricotta cheese makes an excellent base for stuffings. It has a good texture and binding ability and a blandness that is beautifully complemented by the addition of vegetables such as chard, mushrooms, or even zucchini.

6 *Tablespoons butter*   ¼ *cup fresh bread crumbs*
1 *small onion, finely chopped* ¼ *teaspoon nutmeg, or more*
1 *garlic clove, finely chopped*   *to taste*
1 *cup ricotta cheese (250*   *Salt*
   grams)   *Freshly ground black pepper*
3 *Tablespoons sour cream*
1 *cup coarsely chopped,*
   cooked chard, kale, collards,
   spinach, or other bitter
   greens

Melt the butter in a skillet over medium-low heat. When hot, add the onions and garlic, and sauté until tender and translucent, about 4 minutes.

In a mixing bowl, combine the ricotta, sour cream, cooked greens, bread crumbs, and sautéed onions. Mix well. Season with nutmeg, salt, and pepper to taste.

Serve with crisp potatoes, buttered peas, or young green beans, and a crusty homemade bread. A somewhat dry and fruity white wine such as a Riesling from Alsace in France or a Johannisberg Riesling from California would go well with the cheese stuffing.

Makes enough for 1 medium chicken (stuffed in the cavity) or 1 large chicken (stuffed under the skin).

This stuffing is also excellent when sautéed mushrooms or shredded zucchini (squeezed dry and sautéed briefly to remove excess moisture) are substituted for the cooked greens.

For a low-calorie stuffing Michel Guerard suggests a stuffing using ricotta as a base. Use 1 cup of low-fat ricotta, flavor it with 3 tablespoons of low-fat yogurt, a cup of chopped fresh herbs, and salt and pepper. Or, if you wish, replace the herbs with shredded zucchini or cooked and coarsely chopped greens.

MUSHROOM TARRAGON STUFFING

———————— ❖❖❖ ————————

This is a good example of how warm and sweet tarragon and mushrooms taste together.

4 *Tablespoons butter*
1 *small onion, finely chopped*
1 *celery rib, finely chopped*
2 *garlic cloves, finely chopped*
¼ *pound mushrooms, coarsely chopped* (125 grams)

¼ *cup chopped fresh tarragon, or 2 to 3 teaspoons crushed dried tarragon*
1½ *cups fresh bread crumbs*
3 *eggs, well beaten*
Salt
Freshly ground black pepper

Melt the butter in a large skillet over medium-low heat. When hot, add the onions, celery, garlic, and mushrooms, and sauté until tender and translucent, about 6 minutes. Stir in the tarragon and sauté 1 minute longer.

In a large mixing bowl, combine the bread crumbs, sautéed vegetables, and eggs. Mix thoroughly. Season with salt and pepper to taste.

Serve with broccoli or tender peas and baked tomatoes, and an elegant red wine from the Médoc in France's Bordeaux region such as a classed growth from the communes Saint-Estèphe or Saint-Julien.

Makes enough for 1 medium-sized chicken.

CORNBREAD STUFFING

❖❖❖

4 *Tablespoons butter*
½ *medium onion, chopped*
1 *garlic clove, finely chopped*
3 *cups crumbled cornbread*
1 4-*ounce can peeled green*
  chilies, chopped (about 100
  grams)

4 *ounces Monterey Jack*
  cheese, diced (100 grams)
½ *cup canned corn niblets*
6 *Tablespoons sour cream*
2 *eggs, well beaten*
Salt
Freshly ground black pepper

Melt the butter in a skillet over medium-low heat. When hot, add the onion and garlic, and sauté until tender and translucent, about 4 minutes.

In a mixing bowl, combine the cornbread, chilies, cheese, corn niblets, sautéed onions, sour cream, and beaten eggs. Mix well. Taste, and season with salt and pepper.

Serve with a simple green vegetable and a hearty red wine such as a Côtes du Rhône.

Makes enough for 1 large or 2 small chickens.

ROAST SPLIT CHICKEN
(Plain or Stuffed under the Skin)

❖❖❖

MASTER RECIPE

❖

Roasting a split chicken is in many ways better, and takes less time and effort, than roasting a whole chicken. The skin roasts to a deeper, more luscious-looking brown, with a thin crispness that the skin of a whole roasted bird never has. It is beautiful to present at tableside with no more than a few sprigs of fresh parsley or watercress for garnish.

1 2½- to 3-pound chicken at
   room temperature, split
   according to the directions
   on page 233 (1¼–1½
   kilograms)
Stuffing (optional), from any
   of the stuffing recipes on
   pages 22 to 30, or a
   favorite stuffing of your
   choice

10 Tablespoons butter, semisoft but still cold (remove
   from the refrigerator 1
   hour before needed), or ½
   cup oil
Salt
Freshly ground black pepper

This recipe is for a 2½- to 3-pound chicken. For chickens of other weights, consult the roasting chart on page 32 for the exact cooking time.

Preheat oven to 450° F.

For chicken stuffed under the skin, prepare the stuffing and allow it to cool to room temperature.

Split the chicken. Place the chicken on the counter, skin side down. Rub the underside with 2 to 3 tablespoons of the butter or oil, and sprinkle with salt and pepper. Massage the salt and pepper into the oil or butter, much of which will have lodged itself between the bones.

IF STUFFING: Starting at the tail end, carefully slide your fingers under the skin, lifting the skin from the meat across the whole of the back, legs, and thighs. Work slowly and carefully so as not to puncture or tear the skin as you loosen it from the fat that adheres to the back and from the thin membrane that holds it over the legs and thighs. Turn the chicken around, and again using only your fingers, carefully separate the skin from the meat of the breast.

Flatten 2 to 3 tablespoons of the stuffing into a thick patty. Lift the skin and slide the stuffing under it. Repeat until all of the meat has been covered with stuffing. Smooth the skin back into place, gently massaging the stuffing so that it spreads evenly over the meat. Remove any bits of stuffing that are on top of the skin.

WHETHER OR NOT YOU ARE STUFFING THE CHICKEN: Melt the remaining butter if used. Brush the skin lavishly with melted butter or oil and sprinkle with salt and pepper. Place on a rack in a shallow roasting pan. Using a rack allows the heat to circulate evenly around the chicken.

Place the roasting pan on a shelf in the lower third of a preheated oven. This means that the chicken itself is in the middle of the oven.

Roast the chicken for the estimated cooking time, in this case 45 to 50 minutes. Brush generously with butter or oil every 8 to 10 minutes to keep the skin sealed and crisp.

TEST THE CHICKEN FOR DONENESS. After 45 minutes of the roasting time, the low end of the estimated cooking time on the roasting chart, check for doneness (see page 7).

When done, transfer to a warm platter or carving board. Allow the chicken to rest at room temperature for 5 to 10 minutes before carving. This gives the juices a chance to settle back into the meat.

ROASTING CHART
Split Chicken (Stuffed and Unstuffed)

READY-TO-COOK WEIGHT	APPROXIMATE COOKING TIME (IN MINUTES)	
	UNSTUFFED	STUFFED
¾ to 1 pound (350–500 grams)	20 to 25 / 20 to 25	25 to 30 / 25 to 30
1½ to 2 pounds (750–1000 grams)	30 to 35 / 35 to 40	35 to 40 / 40 to 45
2½ to 3 pounds (1¼–1½ kilograms)	40 to 45 / 45 to 55	45 to 50 / 55 to 60
3½ to 4 pounds (1¾–2 kilograms)	45 to 55 / 55 to 65	50 to 60 / 65 to 75
4½ to 5 pounds (2¼–2½ kilograms)	50 to 60 / 70 to 80	55 to 65 / 70 to 80
5½ to 6 pounds (2¾–3 kilograms)	60 to 70 / 75 to 85	65 to 75 / 80 to 90

The rich, buttery pan drippings provide all the sauce needed. Spoon a tablespoon or so over each serving. If you prefer a sauce or gravy to the pan drippings, refer to the notes on page 9. For unstuffed roast chicken, see the vegetable and wine suggestions on page 8. For stuffed chicken, choose the vegetables and wine suggested for the stuffing.

For extra flavor and variation, instead of stuffing, lift the skin as directed on page 31 and rub the meat with any of the flavored butters or oils on pages 10 to 18.

VARIATION

PARSLEYED ROAST CHICKEN: Roast it, unstuffed, as directed in the master recipe, spreading 3 to 4 tablespoons of butter under the skin. When the chicken is done, brush with a thin coating of mustard. Combine ¾ cup fresh bread crumbs with ½ cup chopped parsley and moisten with 6 tablespoons of melted butter. Season with a little salt and freshly ground black pepper. Press a layer of the parsleyed crumbs over the skin of the chicken, and place under a preheated broiler for 2 to 3 minutes to heat the crumbs and to brown them slightly. Watch carefully to be certain the bread crumbs do not burn.

SPIT-ROASTED CHICKEN

———— ❖❖❖ ————

Spit roasting is the oldest form of cooking in the world. The green stick that neolithic man forced through his meat has become the shiny, stainless-steel spit of today's electric rotisserie, but the technique itself has remained unchanged and is still one of the best ways of cooking chicken.

1 *2½- to 3-pound chicken, at*   *Salt*
   room temperature (1¼–   *Freshly ground black pepper*
   1½ kilograms)   *3 or 4 slices of bacon*
8 *Tablespoons butter, semi-*
   soft but still cold (remove
   from the refrigerator 1
   hour before needed)

This recipe is for a 2½- to 3-pound chicken. For chickens of other weights, consult the roasting chart on page 35 for the exact cooking time.

Preheat the oven or rotisserie to 450° F. if the temperature is thermostatically regulated.

Rub the inside of the chicken with 2 tablespoons of the butter or oil, and season with salt and pepper. Truss the chicken (see page 221).

Pat the outside of the chicken thoroughly dry. Spread about half the remaining butter over the outside of the chicken. Sprinkle with salt and pepper, massaging the seasonings into the butter. Melt the remaining butter and reserve for basting.

Blanch the bacon by placing it in boiling water for 1 minute. Drain and pat dry.

Lay the strips of bacon across the chicken so that they cover most of the breast, legs, and thighs. Using kitchen string, tie the bacon securely in place. This may take a bit of patience, as the bacon tends to slide off before you get the next loop of string over it. This barding, as it is called, is important, for it acts as a screen to protect the breast, and it also bastes the chicken as it turns.

Slide a clamp onto the spit and secure it by turning the screw so that it holds in place about two thirds of the way down the spit. Carefully poke the spit into the opening just under the legs, through the cavity of the chicken, and out the neck opening. Press the chicken gently against the prongs of the clamp on the lower end of the spit and slide the second clamp into place. Adjust the clamps so that the chicken is balanced on the spit and is in the center of the oven or rotisserie when the spit is in place and turning. When you are certain that the chicken is properly centered and balanced, press the prongs firmly against the flesh and secure the clamps in place by fully tightening the screws.

SPIT-ROASTED CHICKEN

Ready-to-Cook Weight	Approximate Cooking Time (in minutes)
¾ to 1 pound (350–500 grams)	25 to 30 25 to 30
1½ to 2 pounds (750–1000 grams)	35 to 40 40 to 45
2½ to 3 pounds (1¼–1½ kilograms)	45 to 50 45 to 55
3½ to 4 pounds (1¾–2 kilograms)	50 to 60 55 to 65
4½ to 5 pounds (2¼–2½ kilograms)	55 to 65 65 to 75
5½ to 6 pounds (2¾–3 kilograms)	65 to 75 75 to 85

Place the chicken in the oven or rotisserie, start it turning and roast for two thirds the approximate cooking time, 30 minutes in this case.

Carefully take the chicken out of the oven or rotisserie and remove the bacon to allow the top of the chicken to brown. Brush with butter. Return to the oven or rotisserie and roast until done, basting once or twice more with the remaining butter.

To TEST THE CHICKEN FOR DONENESS: After 45 minutes of roasting, the low end of the estimated cooking time, check for doneness (see page 7).

When done, using a pot holder or heavy towel, loosen the clamps. Slide the chicken off the spit and onto a warm platter or carving board. Remove the trussing string and allow the chicken to rest at room temperature for 10 to 15 minutes before carving. This gives the juices a chance to settle back into the flesh. For carving directions, see page 239.

SAUCE: The drippings that have accumulated in the pan under the chicken are all the sauce needed. Spoon a tablespoon or so over each serving. If you prefer a sauce or gravy to the pan drippings, see the notes on page 9. Serve with any of the vegetables or wines suggested for simple roast chicken on page 8.

2

BROILING AND GRILLING

———— ❖❖❖ ————

$\mathbb{B}$ROILING OR GRILLING, indoors or out, is one of the best and most delicious ways of cooking chicken. But it wasn't always that way. For the eighteenth- and nineteenth-century cook, neither broiling nor grilling was particularly popular, as Mrs. Bradley points out in *The British Housewife* (circa 1770):

The Advantage of Roasting above Broiling is plain, because it is out of the Way of the Smoak; whereas broiled Things are exposed to it, if there be ever so little. It is for this reason that most of those Things we usually broil, eat better roasted. . . .

Broiling and grilling meant the same thing until the late nineteenth century, when broiling became a way of cooking by radiant heat where the heat source was *above* the meat. In 1893 at the Chicago World's Fair, an electric broiler was first introduced to Americans. During the next fifty years, professional broilers were to undergo great improvement, while the increasingly popular domestic versions improved little. Household broilers, especially those built into ovens, simply do not generate enough heat to broil properly. Yet even with its limitations, broiling is the second most popular way of cooking chicken in all regions of this country except the South.

The purpose of cooking by direct, or radiant, heat is to cook the meat quickly: close to the heat source to seal in all of the natural juices and only far enough away from the heat to prevent burning. As a result, the most important part of grilling and broiling is the heat source. And, unfortunately, it is also the greatest variable.

There are certain things about the heat source we can control, regardless of its specific limitations. First, allow the broiler or grill to become fully preheated. In the case of a charcoal grill, this means a full bed of white, ash-laden coals, evenly distributed to the perimeter of the grill. In the case of indoor grills, consult the manufacturer's directions on preheating. If your broiler is part of the oven and not housed in a separate compartment, remember that it must be preheated with the door left slightly ajar or the air in the lower part of the oven will become so hot that it will bake the meat rather than broil it. In addition, bear in mind that gas broilers usually get hotter than electric ones.

When cooking by direct heat, sealing the chicken is the first objective. The first thing that happens when the meat comes into contact with the heat is that the albumin, which is found in all meat as well as egg whites, hardens. If the meat is dry, and there is little or no moisture on the outside surface, the natural sugars will then caramelize, producing a beautiful crisp, golden-brown skin. Both of these reactions help to seal in the natural juices of the meat. To help this sealing process, baste the outside of the meat with a thin coating of oil or melted fat, which acts as a screen, allowing the heat to penetrate into the chicken and preventing the natural juices from escaping as steam. Occasionally little blisters or bubbles appear on the skin during broiling or grilling. This is where the natural juices have turned to steam and stretched the skin in an attempt to escape. If the meat has been well sealed and basted, then the steam has been forced back into the meat, helping to cook it and keeping it moist and tender. Sealing is the basic principle of grilling and broiling. Rubbing the chicken with oil also serves a secondary purpose: it prevents the chicken from sticking to the grill.

In broiling and grilling it is important to regulate the heat so that the chicken is properly and quickly sealed but not burnt. This is done by either raising or lowering the chicken, or in the case of thermostatically controlled broilers or grills, by regulating the temperature of the heat source itself.

Broiled or grilled chicken has a distinctive taste and character that comes from the browning and the intensity of the heat— not, as is often believed, from the taste of the charcoal. There is, however, a way of adding additional flavor to grilled meats that I remember my father using. He would soak hickory-wood chips overnight in a large bucket of cold water and then distribute a handful of the dampened chips over preheated coals. When they began to smoke, it was time to arrange the meat or chicken on the grill. Hickory is a favorite wood for this type of grilled smoking, but there are many other types of sweet wood which are also excellent—maple, oak, alder, apple, and cherry, to name just a few. Remember to distribute the chips judiciously: too much smoke may flavor the chicken too heavily, and too many chips can smother the fire.

SIMPLE GRILLED CHICKEN

❖❖❖

MASTER RECIPE

❖

1 2½- to 3-pound chicken, split or cut in half (see pages 233 and 236), or cut into serving pieces (see page 224) (1¼–1½ kilograms)	Salt Freshly ground black pepper ½ cup oil

Preheat the grill. Some electric grills will preheat in 5 to 10 minutes, others may take longer. For outdoor charcoal grilling, 30 minutes to 1 hour may be needed to obtain a good bed of ashen-white coals.

Pat the chicken dry. Season with salt and pepper, and rub generously with oil. Reserve the remaining oil for basting. Place the chicken, skin side down, on a grill 2 to 3 inches above the heat. Grill 6 to 7 minutes on each side. Baste generously with oil when the chicken is turned. Basting seals the skin and keeps the chicken moist. Always turn with tongs, not with a fork, which will pierce the skin and break the seal. If the skin shows signs of burning, the chicken is too close to the heat.

Raise the grill to about 4 inches from the heat. Grill 10 to 15 minutes longer, turning and basting once or twice more.

(Keep a small bowl of water handy when charcoal grilling. Often the fat dripping from the chicken or the oil used for basting will cause the coals to flare up. Douse the flames with a little water to prevent them from burning the chicken.)

TEST FOR DONENESS: Insert an instantly registering thermometer into the thickest part of the meat, without touching the bone. White meat is cooked when it registers an internal temperature of 140° F., dark meat when it registers 165° F. When white meat is done, remove to a heated platter and keep warm while dark meat finishes grilling.

Chicken that would cook in 20 to 25 minutes over a very hot indoor grill may take as long as 35 to 40 minutes on a cold day over charcoal. As cooking times can vary so much from one grill to another, I suggest you record the cooking time on your grill and use that as a guide whenever you grill chicken. For longer grilling times, turn and baste chicken once or twice more.

Serve grilled chicken with a Béarnaise sauce (page 213) if you wish, French fries, and a mixed green salad. Garnish the plate with cherry tomatoes and a sprig or two of watercress.

A full-bodied and quite elegant red wine would be nice if you're eating indoors in a relatively formal way. But I have visions of being outdoors—sitting on the grass, the hot summer sun just going down—and wanting a very full-bodied though not particularly elegant red wine that could stand up to a charred taste. I'd probably choose an inexpensive Zinfandel from California.

Makes 4 to 6 servings.

Although they are expensive and difficult to find, baby chickens weighing about ¾ pound are excellent for grilling. To grill a baby chicken, split it down the back (see directions on page 233), and grill exactly as you would a regular piece of chicken. Grilled baby chickens are a good way to make a simple meal look and feel very festive.

GRILLED CHICKEN STEAKS

———————— ❖❖❖ ————————

This grilled chicken steak is simple to make. It consists of 2 suprêmes folded together and gently pounded, and sprinkled with lemon juice and salt and pepper. It should be grilled quickly and very close to the heat so that all the tender juiciness of the breast meat is sealed in.

12 *suprêmes (boneless and*	*Salt*
skinless half-breasts, see	*Freshly ground black pepper*
page 233)	*Oil*
½ *lemon*	

Preheat grill to very hot.

Place each suprême between two sheets of waxed paper. With the side of a cleaver or a meat pounder, flatten to just under ¼ inch in thickness. With a sharp knife, trim any ragged edges. Sprinkle with a few drops of lemon juice and season lightly with salt and pepper.

Place a piece of the chicken flat on the counter, the side with the thin, shiny, white membrane down. Place a second piece of chicken, again shiny side down, on top of it so that half of each piece is overlapping. Fold the outside flap of the first piece over the second, making three layers. Finally, fold the remaining flap over the top of the three layers. You now have a rectangular-shaped chicken steak, ¾ to 1 inch thick.

Place this steak between two pieces of waxed paper and gently pound it just into an even thickness. This is not meant to make the steak thinner but only to make it uniform in thickness so that it cooks evenly. Shape the remaining suprêmes in the same way.

Rub the steaks generously with oil. Arrange on a grill over hot coals, about 1½ to 2 inches above the heat. Placed on the hot grill, the steaks should sizzle. Cook for 2½ to 3 minutes and turn them over. Cook for another 2½ to 3 minutes. Turn the steaks again, arranging them on the grill so that the grating is running perpendicular to the way it did before. The markings from the grill should form a decorative pattern on the outside of the steaks. Grill another 2½ to 3 minutes. Turn, again making sure the lines are perpendicular, and grill 2½ to 3 minutes.

Do not overcook the chicken. All that is needed over a very hot grill is 10 to 12 minutes. Test for doneness by inserting an instantly registering thermometer sideways into the center of the steak. The chicken is done when it registers 140° F.

Place the steaks on a heated plate and, if you wish, top with a pat of any of the herbed butters on pages 10–16.

Serve with fried potatoes and a vegetable stew. Most bone-dry white wines or light reds would make a nice accompaniment, but this is such a delicate, pretty dish that you might want a sparkling white wine, perhaps a Champagne if you're feeling rich.

Makes 6 servings.

GRILLED CHINESE CHICKEN WINGS

❖❖❖

If you have the patience to bone the chicken wings, you'll find this a great alternative to feeding the kids hot dogs or hamburgers on your next picnic. And with a little supervision the children can easily grill these themselves.

12 *to* 24 *wings*	*Salt*
Oil	*Freshly ground black pepper*

Bone the wings according to the directions on page 236. This can be done ahead of time. Drape the wings with a damp towel and wrap tightly in plastic wrap. Refrigerate until needed. If transporting them to a picnic, it is best to keep them in the cooler.

Preheat the grill.

Rub the meat and bone with oil, and season the chicken with salt and pepper. Grill about 2 to 3 inches from the heat for 10 to 12 minutes, turning 3 or 4 times.

To serve at a picnic, cool for a minute or two, then simply wrap a paper napkin around the bone and let the nibbling begin.

I don't usually recommend rosé wines, but the kids—those of legal drinking age, of course—would probably love a medium-dry rosé from Portugal, an Anjou rosé from France's Loire Valley, or a rosé of Cabernet Sauvignon from California. In whites, a well-chilled Chénin Blanc would be nice; in reds, a slightly chilled Valpolicella.

Makes 12 to 24 wings.

YAKITORI

———— ❖❖❖ ————

This is a Japanese hors d'oeuvre of marinated chicken skewered with mushrooms and tomatoes. The importance of color and texture in Japanese cooking is beautifully illustrated in this recipe. Whenever meat and vegetables are combined on a skewer, it is important that they all cook in the same time. For that reason, the mushrooms are poached before being skewered with the chicken and tomatoes.

3 *boneless and skinless chicken breasts*	2 *cups chicken stock*
	Juice of ½ a lemon
1 *recipe teriyaki marinade (see page 50)*	36 *to* 48 *cherry tomatoes, or 2 boxes*
48 *to* 72 *small mushroom caps, about* 1½ *pounds* (about 750 grams)	12 *to* 18 *bamboo skewers*

Dice the chicken into 1-inch pieces. There should be 12 to 18 pieces from each breast. Place in the marinade, and marinate 2 to 3 hours.

Cut the stems from the mushrooms (and reserve for making a stock). Combine the stock and lemon juice in a saucepan and bring to a boil. Add the mushroom caps, reduce heat and simmer, turning occasionally, until just barely tender when pierced with a skewer, about 6 to 8 minutes.

Arrange the mushrooms, chicken, and tomatoes on bamboo skewers in the following sequence: Mushroom, tomato, chicken; mushroom, tomato, chicken; and again; and finish with a mushroom. The yakitori can be prepared ahead of time up to this point, wrapped tightly and refrigerated until an hour or so before grilling.

Preheat the grill to very hot.

Dip the skewers into the marinade and arrange on a grill 2 inches above the heat. Grill for 3 to 4 minutes on each side, basting with additional marinade when the skewers are turned. Serve immediately. I think this dish, served in small portions, would make a lovely appetizer to a meal that also contained a heavier or more important main course. In this case, I'd serve the yakitori with a Chardonnay from a very fine, small winery in either California's Napa or Sonoma valleys, or with a very elegant and expensive white Burgundy such as Bâtard Montrachet or a Meursault.

For an informal occasion I'd serve a less expensive version of the same wines, such as a Mâcon Blanc Villages from France or a Chardonnay from California.

Makes 12 to 18 skewers.

These can be broiled rather than grilled, if you wish. For broiling, keep the skewers about 2 to 3 inches from the heat.

SIMPLE BROILED CHICKEN

❖❖❖

MASTER RECIPE

❖

1 2½- to 3-pound chicken, split or cut in half (see pages 233 and 236), or cut into serving pieces (see page 224) (1¼–1½ kilograms)	Salt Freshly ground black pepper ½ cup oil

Preheat the broiler. This will take 5 to 10 minutes and should be done with the door left slightly ajar.

Season chicken with salt and pepper, and rub generously with oil. Reserve remaining oil for basting.

Arrange chicken, skin side up, on a rack over a shallow roasting pan. Place 3 to 4 inches below a preheated broiling unit. Broil 6 to 8 minutes on each side. Baste generously with oil when the chicken is turned. Always turn with a pair of tongs, not with a fork, which will pierce the skin and allow the natural juices of the meat to escape. Baste again, to keep the skin sealed and the chicken moist, and lower the chicken to a distance of 4 to 5 inches from the broiling unit. As gas broilers radiate more heat than electric broilers, chicken should be kept slightly lower in a gas oven. Broil 10 to 15 minutes longer, turning once and basting with the remaining oil. Regulate the distance between the chicken and the broiling unit so that the chicken seals during the first 6 to 8 minutes of cooking on each side, and then continues to cook without burning or blistering too much until done.

Test for doneness (see page 42). Depending on the size and amount of heat radiated from the broiling unit, the size of the oven, and the temperature of the chicken before broiling, the total cooking time may vary from just under half an hour to as much as 45 to 50 minutes. During longer broiling periods, turn and baste the chicken occasionally.

Garnish with watercress or parsley, and serve with mashed or French fried potatoes, and a green vegetable or romaine salad. Should you wish a sauce, a Béarnaise (see page 213) would be excellent.

This dish goes with almost anything, though it sounds sufficiently mundane to be served to a spouse who has worked all day by another spouse who has worked all day and run out of artful kitchen ideas. This would be a good time to serve a jug of fairly dry California wine, either red or white. You might even transfer the wine into a pretty carafe.

Makes 4 to 6 servings.

BROILED DEVILED CHICKEN

—————— ❖❖❖ ——————

1 2½- to 3-pound chicken, cut
  into serving pieces (see
  page 224) (1¼–1½ kilo-
  grams)

DEVILING SAUCE

½ cup Dijon mustard
½ cup oil
¼ cup honey
Juice of 1 lemon
1 teaspoon freshly ground
  black pepper

2 Tablespoons capers, finely
  chopped
6 to 8 garlic cloves, finely
  chopped

TO FINISH

½ cup oil

½ cup dried bread crumbs

Preheat broiler.

Combine the mustard, oil, honey, lemon juice, pepper, capers, and garlic, and mix well. Brush the chicken generously with this deviling sauce.

Arrange chicken on a rack over a shallow roasting pan. Broil for 7 minutes on each side, 3 to 4 inches below the broiler. Chicken should not be more than just slightly charred at this point.

Brush chicken with oil, and roll in bread crumbs. Press the bread crumbs firmly onto the chicken.

Place chicken 4 to 6 inches below the broiling unit and broil 8 to 10 minutes, carefully turning once or twice and watching to see that the bread crumbs do not burn. Test for doneness (see page 42).

Just before serving, either brush lavishly with melted butter or accompany with a mustard-flavored hollandaise (see page 212). Serve with potatoes. This dish is quite a bit more exciting than simple broiled chicken and well worth the effort. After expending this much energy on the recipe, you might like to experiment with a fruity, "spicy" white wine with a slightly sweet finish such as a Gewürztraminer from California, which has both the flavor and robustness to stand up to this dish, or serve it with a full, rich, gutsy Rioja burgundy-style red wine from northern Spain.

Makes 4 to 6 servings.

This recipe is a good way to use about 3 pounds of legs or thighs, or both. The flavor and texture of the dark meat are a particularly good foil for the deviling sauce and crumbs.

MARINADES

———— ❖❖❖ ————

A marinade is a highly flavored liquid in which meat, game, poultry, or fish is soaked, or marinated. It traditionally served two purposes: to flavor the meat and to tenderize it. As today's chickens are designed and bred for tenderness, the only real function of a marinade is for flavoring. A marinade can be as simple as a few drops of lemon juice or it can include a long list of ingredients, often requiring several hours of simmering, or it can be a paste of spices and other ingredients rubbed onto the chicken and then wiped off before cooking.

CURRY MARINADE

———— ❖❖❖ ————

1 *cup chicken stock*
1 *cup water*
1 *cup dry white wine*
1 *medium onion, sliced*
3 *shallots, coarsely chopped (optional)*

1 *ounce fresh ginger, coarsely chopped* (30 grams)
3 *Tablespoons curry powder*
Grated zest of ½ lemon

Combine all ingredients, and mix well. Add chicken and marinate 12 to 24 hours. Turn the chicken and stir the marinade at least once. Grill or broil as directed in the master recipes, pages 41 and 46.

Serve with rice or potatoes, and a mixed green salad.

This marinade is more a curry tantalizer than a firingly spiced dish, so I'd recommend either a full-bodied dry white wine from Italy such as Orvieto, or a medium-bodied, slightly softer and sweeter California white such as Chénin Blanc.

TERIYAKI MARINADE

❖❖❖

1 *cup soy sauce*
⅓ *cup oil*
⅓ *cup sherry*
2 *Tablespoons sugar*
4 *garlic cloves, coarsely chopped*

½ *ounce fresh ginger, coarsely chopped* (15 grams)

Combine all ingredients, and mix well. Add chicken, and marinate 12 to 24 hours, turning the chicken at least once. Grill or broil as directed in the master recipes, pages 41 and 46.

As this dish is marinated in Sherry and contains some potent spices and sugar, I'd suggest a wine that's full yet refreshing, such as a truly fine, bone-dry Fino Sherry from Spain, well chilled. That's if it's a first course. If it's to be your main course, a full-bodied red such as a Côtes du Rhône or Corbières from France would be nice.

SOY AND MADEIRA MARINADE

❖❖❖

This is an interesting variation on the traditional teriyaki marinade, using Madeira instead of Sherry. It can be used in any recipe calling for the teriyaki marinade.

1 *cup oil*
3 *cups soy sauce*
4 *ounces fresh ginger, thinly sliced* (100 grams)

8 *to* 10 *garlic cloves, unpeeled and coarsely chopped*
¾ *cup Madeira*
Juice of 1 *lemon*

Combine all ingredients, and mix well. Add chicken, and marinate 12 to 24 hours, turning chicken at least once. Grill or broil as directed in the master recipes, pages 41 and 46.

Don't be tempted to drink a Madeira with this dish. Madeira is lovely after dinner and with stewed fruits, but it is too sweet to drink with an entrée of chicken. This dish would do better with a fairly fruity red wine such as a Zinfandel from California.

GARLIC AND SAFFRON MARINADE

❖❖❖

So far the marinades in this chapter have been liquids in which the chicken is soaked. This marinade is a paste which is spread on the chicken and then partially wiped off. It's the kind of marinade frequently used in Indian and Middle Eastern cooking. It is delicious, and great for picnics.

1 *large head of garlic, broken into cloves and peeled*
½ *teaspoon saffron*
1 *teaspoon crushed dried oregano*

1 *teaspoon salt*
1 *teaspoon freshly ground pepper*
Oil

Combine all the ingredients except the oil in a blender or food processor, and purée to form a smooth, bright yellow paste.

Rub the outside of the chicken with this paste and marinate for 2 hours at room temperature. Just before broiling or grilling, moisten the chicken with about ½ cup of oil, rubbing off any bits of excess paste. Mix some additional oil with the excess marinade and use for basting.

Grill or broil as directed in the master recipes, pages 41 and 46.

Serve with rice and a crisp green salad. A hearty red wine such as a Beaujolais from the villages of Fleurie or Morgan would be lovely, as would a full-bodied Barolo of Italy's Piedmont.

BARBECUE SAUCES

❖❖❖

A barbecue sauce can act as both a marinade and a basting sauce, depending on how much barbecued flavor you want on your chicken. They can be as easy to make as the Uncooked Barbecue Sauce, taking only a few seconds to mix together a half-dozen ingredients, or they can be more complicated, taking many hours of simmering, with a multitude of ingredients to be added at different times. They all seem to bring to mind a universal dark red-brown color and basic taste. Whether using one of the barbecue sauces here or your own favorite, don't use too much. You still want to taste the chicken underneath it.

When using one of the barbecue sauces suggested below, grill or broil according to the directions for grilled chicken, page 41, or broiled chicken, page 46.

UNCOOKED BARBECUE SAUCE

❖❖❖

¾ *cup Worcestershire Sauce*   ¼ *cup oil*
¾ *cup brown sugar*   1 *teaspoon salt*
6 *Tablespoons red wine*   ½ *teaspoon freshly ground*
  vinegar   *black pepper*
3 *Tablespoons chili powder*   6 *Tablespoons tomato paste*

Combine all ingredients, and mix well. Makes about 2 cups. Use for broiled or grilled chicken; serve with beer.

ONION BARBECUE SAUCE

———— ❖❖❖ ————

¼ *cup oil*
1 *large onion, finely chopped*
1 *cup tomato purée*
Juice of 2 lemons
⅔ *cup Worcestershire Sauce*
¼ *cup soy sauce*
¼ *cup brown sugar*

2 *teaspoons salt*
1 *teaspoon freshly ground*
  black pepper
4 *teaspoons (1 Tablespoon*
  plus 1 teaspoon) paprika
1 *teaspoon Tabasco Sauce*

Place the oil in a large saucepan over medium-high heat. When hot, add the onion and sauté until nicely browned but not burnt, about 3 to 4 minutes. Mix the remaining ingredients and add to the onions. Reduce heat and simmer 15 minutes. Makes about 3 cups.

Use for grilled or broiled chicken (see pages 41 and 46); serve with beer or a well-chilled rosé wine.

···3···

POACHING, BRAISING, FRICASSEEING, AND STEWING

Boiling is the Dressing Things by
Means of Water, as Roasting does it by the
naked Fire; this is the whole Difference, but in general
Boiling is the easiest Way, as it requires
less Nicety and Attendance.

MRS. BRADLEY,
The British Housewife (c. 1770)

MAN LEARNED TO CONTROL fire about 500,000 B.C., and it seems reasonable for food historians to assume that roasting was accidentally discovered soon after that. The next major advance in culinary technique was the development of cooking by moist heat. It took almost half a million years for man to learn to boil meat because boiling water very rarely occurs in nature, and so a technique for boiling had to be developed. To boil water one needs a heat source, water, and a heatproof and watertight container. The heat source was available and certainly there was water, but for almost half a million years there was no practical way of making containers. Not until about 5000 B.C. was man able to produce ceramic cooking vessels, and it was to be another three thousand years before he learned to fashion cauldrons out of bronze.

Something to remember when buying or examining stockpots, braising pans, and the like, is that the shape of the pot is far more important than the metal it is made of. It's the water, not the pot, that conducts and distributes the heat, and water conducts heat just as well in a thin, cheap pot as it does in a heavy, expensive, decoratively trimmed piece of French hammered copper that you can barely lift when empty, let alone when filled to the brim with stock. For poaching and braising chicken I find that the best pots are oval, as they conform closely to the shape of the bird. For fricassees and stews the best shape pot is round with straight sides, thin but sturdy, and 3 to 5 inches in height. I like sturdy pots with heavy aluminum- or copper-clad bottoms, and pots that are easy to clean, preferably stainless steel. Choose a pot that is just large enough to comfortably hold the chicken when completely submerged in liquid. This is important because during the hour or so that it takes to poach the chicken, some of its flavor will be given off into the liquid, and at the same time some of the flavor of the liquid will be absorbed by the chicken. The less excess liquid there is, the better-tasting the chicken will be, and the more flavorful the resulting broth.

The four basic methods of moist cooking are poaching, braising, fricasseeing, and stewing.

Poaching—and for our purposes here, poaching and boiling are the same—is a technique for cooking chicken in which the bird is completely submerged in a simmering (between 190° F.–200° F.) liquid, the surface of which shows a gentle ebullition, a slight movement or occasional rumble from a bubble rising to the surface. To poach a chicken properly requires an understanding of the principles involved. First, the chicken must be trussed. This is simply to hold it in shape during the poaching and to make the bird attractive and appealing when served.

The second principle of poaching is to seal in as much of the natural flavor of the chicken as possible. Occasionally, as in the recipe for Lemon Chicken, the chicken is browned before poaching. Although browning is usually an important way to seal in the flavor of a food, it is rarely used in poaching because the chicken is sealed by immersion. When lowering the chicken in the poaching liquid, bear in mind that there is a natural air pocket in the cavity of the chicken. This will cause the chicken to float unless the air pocket is allowed to fill when the chicken is lowered into the pot. And, of course, when removing the chicken from the poaching liquid, remember to drain the cavity.

The third principle of poaching is to cook the chicken as rapidly as possible in order to maintain the most flavor and preserve the texture and moistness of the chicken. Rapidly boiling water would certainly cook the chicken faster than simmering water, but unfortunately boiling water is too violent and abrasive. Simmering liquid, just below the boiling point, is best.

All of these principles are clearly illustrated by the master recipe for poached chicken. The recipes that follow it use the same basic technique, but different seasonings and garnishes.

Braising is a variation on poaching, with two important differences—the chicken is sealed by browning and the meat is partially, not completely, submerged in the braising liquid. In braising, since there is a greater exchange of flavors between the liquid and the chicken, a bed of sautéed vegetables called a *mirepoix* is added to the liquid to flavor the meat. Less liquid is used so that the meat is partially cooked by the steam, which penetrates better than simmering liquid.

All of the principles of poaching apply to braising: (1) trussing, to hold the chicken in shape; (2) sealing, done by browning rather than immersion in boiling liquid; and (3) rapid cooking, partially from simmering liquid and partially from steaming.

Fricasseeing is a cross between sautéing and poaching. In a fricassee, first the chicken is sautéed, then liquid is added and the chicken finishes cooking as though it were being poached. Finally, the liquid is made into a sauce, a garnish is prepared, and all are combined and reheated.

The first principle of fricasseeing is sealing, which is accomplished by sautéing the chicken. In fricasseeing, the sauté process not only seals the meat but half cooks it as well. There are two ways to sauté chicken, white and brown. In a white sauté, the chicken develops only the faintest sign of coloring, and the exposed flesh becomes white and plump. A brown sauté is done over higher heat and gives the chicken a rich, golden-brown color. The principle of cooking the chicken as rapidly as possible remains, and though the chicken is half-cooked during the sealing process, it is still important to submerge the chicken in boiling liquid and to keep it at a comfortable simmer throughout the cooking.

With a fricassee, cooking the chicken is only half the recipe. Once the chicken is cooked, the fricassee has to be constructed. The poaching liquid has to be reduced to concentrate its flavor, strained, and then thickened. The garnish, which varies significantly from one recipe to another, has to be prepared, and then the whole dish must be decoratively arranged, or composed, and reheated.

The final section of this chapter deals with stewing, an extended form of poaching used to tenderize an old hen or cock. Always truss the chicken if you stew it whole. Sealing becomes unimportant because the cooking time has been extended to break down the fibers of the meat, and the flesh is rich enough to still be flavorful after several hours of stewing. During the stewing process the liquid should be kept as close to a simmer as possible, though if it occasionally boils or becomes a little brisk, it won't hurt the bird. In braising and fricasseeing, the vegetables were sautéed to bring out their flavor before they were added to the liquid. This is not necessary in a stew, where the cooking time is sufficiently long to allow the flavor of the vegetables to mellow and blend without being sautéed.

As hard as some writers have tried to dress stews in expensive wines and elaborate garnishes, a chicken stew just isn't elegant eating.

WHOLE POACHED CHICKEN

❖❖❖

MASTER RECIPE

❖

Poaching is an excellent way of cooking chicken. It respects the integrity and texture of the meat, keeps the chicken flavorful and moist, and requires less effort than roasting. Its one drawback is that poaching doesn't produce crisp skin. But it is by far the best way to cook chicken to be eaten cold, or to be served hot with either a basic white sauce or a rich cream sauce and buttered noodles or rice.

1 2½- to 3- *pound chicken*	*A pot just large enough to*
(1¼–1½ kilograms)	*hold the chicken*
Chicken stock	*comfortably*

This recipe is for a 2½- to 3-pound chicken. For chickens of other weights, consult the poaching chart on page 62.

Remove any excess fat from the vent of the chicken. Truss the chicken (see page 221) to hold it in shape during the cooking. One of the most unattractive sights is a chicken which has been poached without trussing. The chicken looks like it has been tortured to death, its legs spread-eagled to the handles of the pot and its body pulled out of shape.

The chicken ready, choose a pot that is just large enough to hold the chicken when completely immersed in stock. Pour enough stock into the pot to completely immerse the chicken. Bring the stock to a full rolling boil over medium-high heat. Slowly slide the chicken into the stock, neck end first. Hold the legs just above the surface of the water until the cavity of the bird fills with stock. Otherwise an air pocket will form and the chicken will float on top of the stock, the breast protruding above the surface.

When the stock comes back to a boil, reduce the heat to low and simmer, partially covered, for 45 minutes, the low end of the recommended cooking time.

TEST THE CHICKEN FOR DONENESS. Lift the chicken partially out of the pot so that the legs and thighs are above the water. I usually stick a fork under the trussing string around the legs to do this. Insert an instantly registering thermometer into the thickest part of the thigh without touching the bone. Be certain that none of the stock is touching the exposed rod of the thermometer. The chicken is done when the thermometer registers 165° F. If the chicken has not reached that temperature, slide it back into the stock and simmer for 5 minutes longer. Test again.

When done, carefully lift out the chicken, allowing the stock that has filled the cavity to drain back into the pot. Place the chicken on a carving board or heated platter and remove the trussing string. Allow the chicken to rest for 5 to 10 minutes before carving. This gives the natural juices of the chicken a chance to settle into the meat. For carving directions, see page 239.

Serve hot or cold. If serving cold, it is best to allow the chicken to cool completely at room temperature, rather than refrigerate it.

If the chicken is to be eaten hot, serve it with any of the sauces recommended on pages 199 to 217. It is a good idea to prepare the roux for the sauce while the chicken is poaching, and then to reduce and strain the poaching liquid into it while the chicken is resting.

Hot poached chicken can be preceded by a cup of the broth in which the bird was poached (perhaps reduced slightly to concentrate its flavor), strained, and seasoned with salt and pepper.

Accompany the chicken with buttered noodles, rice cooked in broth, boiled potatoes, or thinly sliced carrots cooked in stock while the chicken is poaching. The chicken can also be accompanied by any simple green vegetable, or a nice romaine or chicory salad for a contrast of flavor and texture.

I'd serve this dish with a not-terribly-acidic white wine such as a Pouilly-Fumé or a Sancerre from France's Loire Valley, or a Chénin Blanc from California. However, this is a fairly versatile dish and you may prefer a light red wine such as a Beaujolais from France or a light-bodied Zinfandel from California. The proprietor of famed Château d'Yquem, Marquis

POACHING CHART

Ready-to-Cook Weight	Recommended Poaching Time (in minutes)
¾ to 1 pound (350–500 grams)	25 to 30 25 to 30
1½ to 2 pounds (750–1000 grams)	35 to 40 35 to 45
2½ to 3 pounds (1¼–1½ kilograms)	45 to 50 50 to 60
3½ to 4 pounds (1¾–2 kilograms)	50 to 60 55 to 65
4½ to 5 pounds (2¼–2½ kilograms)	55 to 65 65 to 75
5½ to 6 pounds (2¾–3 kilograms)	70 to 80 80 to 90
Fowl	45 minutes per pound

Alexandre de Lur Saluces, once served me his wine—a rich, full, concentrated and extremely sweet golden wine of France's Sauternes region—with a poached chicken. Because the wine's sweetness was balanced by acidity and had enormous complexity, it was lovely. So let your palate be your guide.

As with any basic preparation, there are hundreds of little variations on poached chicken. The giblets can be poached with the chicken, chopped, and added to a white sauce. A piece of onion, some garlic, some fresh herbs, or a wedge or two of lemon can be placed in the cavity of the chicken for extra flavor. A few tablespoons of tarragon or basil or thyme or rosemary can be added to the poaching liquid, then strained, and fresh herbs added just before serving.

If you are out of chicken stock, plain water can be used, though the resulting broth won't be nearly so flavorful. Actually, poaching a chicken in water is a good way of making stock, or of turning a stock into soup for a later use (see Chapter 8).

Poaching is one of the best ways to cook a fowl. Poach the fowl as directed in this recipe, allowing about 45 minutes of simmering per pound. When done, the meat should feel tender when pierced with a fork but should not be falling off the bones.

These cooking times are based on chickens at room temperature, poached at sea level. For refrigerated chickens, add 5 to 10 minutes to the recommended cooking time. If cooking at high altitudes, the stock will simmer at lower temperatures, and it will be necessary to increase the cooking time accordingly.

LEMON CHICKEN

———— ❖❖❖ ————

This is a cooking-school recipe of James Beard's that never seemed to earn the favored status I think it deserves.

2 *lemons*	1 *teaspoon salt*
1 3½- to 4-*pound chicken*	½ *teaspoon freshly ground*
(1½–1¾ kilograms)	*black pepper*
3 *Tablespoons oil*	*Boiling chicken stock*
1 *large onion, finely chopped*	2 *cans (about ¾ pound each)*
4 *garlic cloves, finely chopped*	*chickpeas* (about 350 grams
2 *teaspoons turmeric*	each)

Cut a ¼-inch-thick slice from the center of one of the lemons. Remove any excess fat from the vent of the chicken and rub with the lemon juice. Squeeze the lemons, strain the juice, and reserve. Truss (see page 221).

Pour the oil into a pot (large enough to comfortably hold the chicken) and place over medium-low heat. When hot, add the onion and garlic; sauté, stirring occasionally, until tender and translucent, about 4 minutes. Stir 1 teaspoon of the turmeric into the onion, and sprinkle with the salt and pepper. Cook for 1 minute longer. Rub the chicken with the remaining 1 teaspoon of turmeric.

Slightly increase the heat under the onions and add the chicken. Sear it for a minute or so on each side until it is golden-yellow all around. It may be necessary to hold the chicken in some clumsy positions to do this. When the chicken is nicely colored, pour enough boiling stock into the pot to almost cover the chicken. Toss the drained chickpeas around the chicken, add the reserved lemon juice, and bring the stock back to a boil. Reduce the heat and simmer until done, about 50 to 60 minutes. Test for doneness (see page 61).

When done, transfer the chicken to a carving board and re-move the trussing string. Allow the chicken to rest for 5 to 10 minutes before carving. Serve with the accompanying chickpeas and onions, moistened with a little of the lemon-flavored broth, and parsleyed potatoes.

This elegant but somewhat gutsy dish deserves a wine in its own league, both in weight and character. I would therefore recommend a fairly full-bodied but elegant red wine such as a Pommard from Burgundy, a Saint-Émilion from Bordeaux or a Pinot Noir or full-bodied Zinfandel from California.

MOROCCAN POACHED CHICKEN
(Djej M'Kalli)

❖❖❖

This is a traditional Moroccan dish—a chicken is bathed in a spicy marinade, and then gently poached the next day. The chicken turns bright yellow, from the turmeric and saffron, and is accompanied by a sauce made from the poaching liquid. Couscous would be the traditional accompaniment, though rice cooked in stock flavored with some lemon juice and garnished with some chopped black olives is also delicious with *Djej M'Kalli.*

1 3- *to 4-pound chicken* (about 2 kilograms)	8 *Tablespoons butter*
4 *garlic cloves*	2 *large onions, very finely chopped*
2 *Tablespoons salt*	2 *garlic cloves, finely chopped*
1 *cup oil*	½ *small lemon, thinly sliced*
2 *teaspoons ginger*	*Chicken stock*
1 *teaspoon turmeric*	3 *Tablespoons butter*
1 *teaspoon freshly ground black pepper*	3 *Tablespoons flour*
¼ *teaspoon saffron*	*Salt*
	Freshly ground black pepper

Remove any excess fat from the chicken.

Smash the garlic cloves with the side of a cook's knife, peel, and combine with the salt in a mortar. Pound to a paste with a pestle. Rub the chicken generously with the garlic paste, and let it stand at room temperature for 1 hour.

Combine the oil, ginger, turmeric, pepper, and saffron. Wipe the garlic off the chicken, and rub with the oil mixture.

Place the chicken in a pot just large enough to comfortably

hold it for poaching. Pour the remaining oil mixture over the chicken. Cover, and refrigerate overnight. It's a good idea to turn the chicken once or twice while it is marinating in the oil mixture.

Remove the chicken and truss (see page 221). Discard the marinade, add the butter to the empty pot, and place over medium heat. When hot, add the onions and chopped garlic, and sauté until tender and wilted, about 6 minutes. It may be necessary to lower the heat slightly to prevent browning. Add the lemon, and enough chicken stock so that it will cover the chicken completely. When the chicken stock has come to a boil, gently lower the chicken into the pot. Reduce the heat and simmer, partially covered, for 50 to 60 minutes. Test the chicken for doneness (see page 61).

While the chicken is poaching, prepare a roux for the sauce. Melt the butter in a saucepan over medium-low heat. When hot, stir in the flour and simmer 3 to 4 minutes, stirring occasionally. Set aside to cool.

When done, place the chicken on a heated platter or carving board. Remove the trussing string and allow the chicken to rest while you prepare the sauce. Strain 4 cups of the poaching liquid into a saucepan and place over medium-high heat. Reduce to about 2 cups. This should take about 6 to 8 minutes. Stir the reduced liquid into the roux, place over medium heat and bring back to a boil, stirring occasionally. When the sauce comes to a boil and is completely thickened, taste, and season with salt and pepper. Pour into a sauceboat, and pass with the chicken.

Serve with couscous or rice.

Certainly, if you could find it in the United States, a full-bodied, almost burnt-tasting, extremely robust red wine from Algeria, Morocco's next-door neighbor, would be nice—as would a similar wine from Morocco itself. Unfortunately, wines from these countries are not yet widely available in the United States. However, a robust red wine from France's Côtes du Rhône would be lovely, as would a full-bodied red wine from Spain's Rioja.

Makes 6 to 8 servings.

The marinade in this recipe is also perfect for grilling or broiling. Cut the chicken into serving pieces, marinate overnight, and then grill or broil as directed in the recipe for grilled chicken, page 41, or broiled chicken, page 46.

BOILED DINNER
(a *Pot au Feu* or a *Bollito Misto*)

❖❖❖

James Beard would call this recipe a Boiled Dinner. Julia Child would think of it as a *Pot au Feu*. To Marcella Hazan, it is a *Bollito Misto*. For my own part, I prefer to remain, at least as far as this recipe is concerned, a man without a country. Call it what you may, they all mean the same thing. And if you really want to topple the towers of ethnic cooking, add a Polish sausage to it.

This enormous meal in itself will take 4 to 5 hours for the preparation and cooking.

THE MEATS

A 3- to 4-pound rump roast, piece of bottom round or brisket (about 1½ kilograms)
1 baby beef tongue, about 3 pounds (about 1¼ kilograms)

1 chicken, weighing from 2½ to 4 pounds (1–2 kilograms)
1 sausage—a cotechino, a lightly smoked sausage from Provence, or perhaps a kielbasy

THE BROTH

Chicken stock
3 to 4 carrots, sliced
2 to 3 celery ribs, sliced
2 medium onions, cut in half
2 garlic cloves
1 bay leaf, crumbled

A few sprigs parsley
2 teaspoons crushed dried thyme
1 Tablespoon salt
1 teaspoon freshly ground black pepper

VEGETABLE ACCOMPANIMENT
(choose 2 to 4 vegetables, depending on availability):

Small new potatoes, 2 to 3 per person

Pearl onions, 2 or 3 per person

Turnips, carved into pieces the size of the onions, 2 or 3 per person

Carrots, carved into lozenge shapes, about 1½ inch long, 2 or 3 per person

Leeks, white part only, 1 or 2 per person

Fresh fennel, cut into quarters or eighths, depending on their size, 2 or 3 wedges per person

Trim any excess fat from the beef. Remove the fat and gristle from the base of the tongue. Pull the excess fat from the vent of the chicken, and truss (see page 221).

Choose a stockpot or kettle large enough to comfortably hold all of the meats and vegetables with a generous amount of stock to cover them. I use a 12-quart pot. Add the stock (and remember there has to be enough liquid to cover all of the meats and vegetables), the vegetables, and the seasonings. Cover, and bring to a boil over medium-high heat. Add the beef, bring the stock back to a boil, then reduce the heat and simmer, partially covered.

Half an hour after putting in the beef, add the tongue. Cook the tongue for an hour, then remove and cool slightly under cold running water so it can be handled easily. Cut through the skin around the base of the tongue and peel it off as though you were removing a glove. Trim any gristle that still remains at the base of the tongue and return it to the pot.

Simmer vegetable accompaniments in a separate pot, using some of the stockpot broth. As each vegetable will require a different amount of cooking time, I like to cook them separately. As soon as they are barely tender, cool under cold running water and set aside. They will be added to the kettle for reheating later. Return the stock to the pot.

When the beef has cooked for about 3 hours, add the chicken. The chicken will need about an hour to cook, depending on its size. Consult the poaching chart (page 62) for a more exact estimate.

Add the sausage for the final 20 to 30 minutes of cooking. If using a cotechino, or other fatty sausage, simmer it in a separate pot with some of the broth from the kettle, then set it aside and discard the broth.

(Let's review the cooking times as it is important that the meats finish cooking at about the same time. The beef needs the longest cooking, about 4 hours. The tongue will need 3 to 3½ hours. The chicken about an hour, depending on its size. The sausage about 20 minutes. Should any of the meats finish ahead of schedule, remove and set aside in some of the broth until the remaining meats are tender.)

When all of the meats are cooked, remove them from the kettle. Strain the broth into a bowl through a large sieve or colander lined with cheesecloth. While the broth is straining, rinse the inside of the pot and wipe dry. Remove all of the fat that rises to the top of the broth. Taste the broth, and season with salt and pepper.

Return the broth to the pot and bring back to a boil. Add all of the meats and vegetable accompaniments, and simmer for 10 to 15 minutes to reheat. The final reheating can be done at any time, so this dish can be made well ahead. If preparing this recipe ahead, it is a good idea to keep the cooked meats and vegetables in the broth to prevent them from drying out.

To begin this meal, serve a cup or bowl of the cooking broth from the kitchen. The meats and vegetables will keep warm in the pot from the temperature of the broth, so just cover the kettle, turn off the heat, and forget about it while you enjoy the broth with your guests.

For the main course, if you have an enormous stockpot that is decorative, or at least attractive, by all means bring it into the dining room. Arrange the meats on a large board, carve, and serve each person a slice or two from each meat and some vegetables moistened with a little broth. A little coarse salt and an excellent mustard is all that will be needed, though a green sauce (see page 214) could also be served.

With this kind of boiled dinner, a large part of your wine selection will depend on who's coming to dinner. If it's just the family, serve fruity, full-bodied California reds such as Cabernet Sauvignon or Zinfandel, which are very nice and can be found in a medium-price range. But if you're having "important" company, by all means splurge on something truly special. This kind of boiled dinner simply isn't served often enough, so it's worth choosing a wine you'll remember as long as you remember the dinner itself. I'd say a red wine with a beautiful bouquet, great balance, and a long, lingering aftertaste. Any number of classed growths from Bordeaux from a good vintage of at least several years old—such as 1964, 1967, or 1970—would be perfect.

This is the largest recipe in this book. It will easily serve 15 or 16 people, and you will still have a nice stockpile of leftovers for the rest of the week.

POULE-AU-POT

❖❖❖

I want there to be no peasant in my
kingdom so poor that he is unable to have a chicken
in his pot (*poule-au-pot*) on Sundays.

HENRY IV OF FRANCE (1553–1610)

When Henry declared his culinary aspiration for the French people, he was not thinking of them just eating a poached chicken once a week. What he had in mind was a boiled dinner (a *pot au feu*), to which a stuffed fowl was added, and which might well have fed the family for the better part of the next week.

Should you wish to fulfill Henry's gastronomic desire, prepare the boiled dinner above, but substitute a stuffed fowl—any of the stuffings on pages 22 to 30, except the oyster stuffing, can be used—for the chicken, and plan about 3 to 4 hours cooking time for the fowl.

POULET DEMI-DEUIL

❖❖❖

Poulet demi-deuil is a chicken studded under the skin with slices of fresh black truffles and very, very gently poached. It is un-questionably the most extravagant and expensive recipe in this book. If you love food, and can find and afford an ounce or two of fresh truffles, this is the perfect dish for a very small, intimate dinner for 2 to 4 persons quietly and luxuriously celebrating Christmas Eve or welcoming in the New Year.

1 2- to 2½-*pound chicken*	*Homemade chicken stock*
(1 kilogram)	*(see page 188)*
1 *ounce* fresh *truffles*	*Maldon, kosher, or coarse-*
(30–50 grams)	*grained sea salt*

Beginning at the neck end of the chicken, gently slide your fingers under the skin, separating the skin from the breast, and then from the thighs and legs. Be very careful not to pierce the skin.

Fresh truffles sold in America are usually "ready-to-cook." However, if all of the earth has not been removed, brush clean and rinse quickly in cold water. Cut into thin slices.

Lift the skin and carefully slip a few slices of truffle onto the legs and thighs. Slide the remaining slices over as much of the breast as possible. Smooth the skin down over the truffles, and truss the chicken (see page 221).

Place a rack on the bottom of a pot just large enough to comfortably hold the chicken. Place the chicken on the rack. In a separate pan, bring to a boil enough stock to cover the chicken. Pour down the side of the pot, not over the chicken, and place over medium-high heat. Just as the stock is about to come back to the boil, reduce the heat and simmer *for 15 minutes,* partially covered. Remove from the heat, cover tightly, and leave chicken in the broth for *exactly 20 minutes.*

Carefully pour off the broth. Place the chicken on a platter or carving board, and remove the trussing string. Allow the chicken to rest for 5 to 10 minutes. Either halve or quarter the chicken, serve with a white sauce made from stock and cream and enriched with egg yolks (see page 203), and accompany with a mixed julienne of fresh vegetables.

If you're having this dish for Christmas or New Year's Eve, serve Champagne. Even better, if you can find it, a rosé Champagne from France would be exquisite. If you can't find this, get a bottle of *brut* Champagne, possibly even a vintage, from any of the leading Champagne houses. If you prefer still wines, that is, nonsparkling, a supremely elegant and perfectly balanced white such as Le Montrachet from France's Burgundy would be superb. And if you prefer reds, an extremely distinguished Saint-Émilion would be lovely.

This is the kind of meal that can comfortably begin with fresh oysters and end with a feathery light, hot lemon soufflé.

Makes 2 to 4 servings.

BRAISED CHICKEN

❖❖❖

MASTER RECIPE

❖

Braising is a process in which the flavor of the meat enriches the braising liquid, in exchange for which the aromatic flavor of the braising liquid is absorbed into the meat. To fully accomplish this, braising is a long, slow process and requires a cut of meat that can handle several hours of cooking without falling apart. Small chickens cook too quickly for much exchange to occur.

MIREPOIX

8 *Tablespoons butter*
1 *whole stalk of celery, very*
   thinly sliced
1 *medium onion, thinly sliced*
2 *garlic cloves, finely chopped*
½ *teaspoon crushed dried*
   rosemary

½ *teaspoon crushed dried*
   thyme
1 *teaspoon salt*
¼ *teaspoon freshly ground*
   black pepper

THE CHICKEN

3 *Tablespoons oil*
1 4- *to* 4½-*pound chicken*
   (1¾–2 kilograms)

1 *cup dry white wine*
2 *to* 3 *cups chicken stock*

Preheat oven to 375° F.

Melt the butter over medium-low heat in a pot just large enough to comfortably hold the chicken. When hot, add the celery, onion, garlic, rosemary, thyme, salt and pepper. Cook the *mirepoix*, stirring occasionally, for 15 to 20 minutes without browning it. This is to bring out the flavor of the vegetables.

While the vegetables are cooking, pour the oil into a large skillet over medium heat. Pat the chicken thoroughly dry. This will help the chicken brown quickly and evenly. Truss (see page 221). Brown the chicken in the hot oil until it is a glistening mahogany color on all sides. It may be necessary to hold the chicken in some awkward positions to do this.

Arrange the celery in a thin layer across the bottom of the pot, the bulk of the celery being mounded around the sides of the pot. Place the chicken, breast side up, in the center of the pot. Add the wine, and enough stock to come about a third of the way up the side of the chicken.

Place the chicken in the oven, partially covered, and braise for 15 minutes. Remove the pot from the oven and carefully turn the chicken onto its side. Braise for 25 minutes. Turn the chicken onto its other side, and braise for another 25 minutes. Now, place the chicken on its back again, breast up, and braise, uncovered, for 20 to 30 minutes, basting once or twice with the braising liquid.

Turning the chicken helps keep it moist, and keeps as much of the chicken as possible submerged in the braising liquid so it can absorb the celery flavor.

TEST FOR DONENESS: Insert an instantly registering thermometer into the thickest part of the thigh without touching the bone. The thermometer should register 165° F. If not, braise the chicken for another 5 to 10 minutes, and test again.

When done, place the chicken on a heated platter, remove the trussing string, and allow it to rest for 5 to 10 minutes before carving. Strain the celery and place it around the chicken. Garnish by sprinkling the celery with chopped parsley or arranging some fresh watercress around the platter. Taste the strained juices, and season with salt and pepper. Pass separately in a warmed sauceboat.

Serve with the accompanying celery and boiled potatoes. This braised chicken could be nice with a simple Beaujolais, slightly chilled if you're in the mood for a red wine, but my preference would be for a dry white with a little fruitiness in the bouquet such as a Pouilly-Fumé or Muscadet, both from the Loire Valley in France.

VARIATIONS

CHICKEN BRAISED WITH MIXED VEGETABLES: Substitute 1 large onion, 2 cups of carrots, and 2 cups of celery, cut in fine julienne, for the sliced celery.

CHICKEN BRAISED WITH FENNEL: Substitute 3 or 4 large bulbs of fresh fennel for the celery. Garnish with chopped fresh dill. Add ¼ cup Pernod to the stock, if you wish.

Any number of variations are possible in preparing the *mirepoix*. A few ideas are suggested above, but 4 to 5 cups of any aromatic vegetable or combination of vegetables, flavored appropriately with herbs or spices, can be used. Also, the chicken can be marinated before braising. The curry marinade (page 49), the garlic and saffron marinade (page 51), or the marinade used in the Jugged Chicken recipe (page 132) would all be good with braised chicken.

BASIC WHITE
CHICKEN FRICASSEE

—————— ❖❖❖ ——————

MASTER RECIPE

—— ❖ ——

A fricassee is a cross between a sauté and a stew. The chicken is cut into pieces, sautéed in butter—a process which partially cooks the chicken—then submerged in a cooking liquid and simmered. The liquid is reduced to concentrate its flavor, strained, and thickened. Finally, the chicken is reheated in the sauce, garnished, and served.

Fricasseeing does take a little bit of work, but the final taste is so rich and lovely, so flattering, that it is well worth the effort.

FOR SAUTÉING

4 *Tablespoons butter or oil*

1 *small onion, thinly sliced*

1 *small carrot, thinly sliced*

½ *celery rib, thinly sliced*

1 *small leek, if available, white part only, thinly sliced*

1 *garlic clove, finely chopped*

1 2½ - *to 3-pound chicken, cut into serving pieces, or 3 pounds of chicken in pieces* (1¼–1½ *kilograms*)

THE SAUCE

3 *cups chicken stock*

1 *cup dry white wine*

Salt

Freshly ground black pepper

3 *Tablespoons butter*

3 *Tablespoons flour*

1 *cup heavy cream*

2 *egg yolks*

Juice of ½ small lemon

Salt

Freshly ground black pepper

Chopped parsley for garnish

SAUTÉING: Melt the butter over medium-low heat in a straight-sided skillet large enough to hold all the chicken pieces in one layer. When the butter is hot, add the onion, carrot, celery, leek if available, and garlic. Sauté until tender but not browned, stirring occasionally, for 5 to 6 minutes. This is to help bring out the flavor of the vegetables. Using a slotted spoon, transfer the sautéed vegetables to a saucepan.

Arrange the chicken pieces in the skillet, skin side down, and sauté, still over a medium-low heat, for 6 to 8 minutes, turning frequently. The chicken should not brown but only take on a light golden hue, with the exposed parts of the flesh turning white and plumping slightly. In gastronomic jargon this is called a white sauté.

THE COOKING: While the chicken is sautéing, add the stock and wine to the saucepan with the vegetables, and bring to a boil over medium-high heat. Taste, and season lightly with salt and pepper. Do not overseason; the liquid will be reduced after the chicken has cooked in it.

After sautéing the chicken, pour the boiling stock and vegetables over it. The chicken should be submerged. If it is not, add a little more stock or white wine. Cover the skillet, reduce the heat to low, and simmer for 20 minutes. Test for doneness.

TESTING THE CHICKEN FOR DONENESS: Remove a piece of the breast from the skillet. Insert an instantly registering thermometer into the thickest part of the meat without touching he bone. It should register 140° F. If not, return the chicken to the skillet and simmer for 5 minutes longer, then test again. When the white meat is done, arrange it on a plate, and drape loosely with aluminum foil to keep it warm while the dark meat finishes cooking. The dark meat will need another 5 to 10 minutes of cooking; it should register 165° F. When done, transfer dark meat to the plate with the white meat.

THE SAUCE: Increase the heat under the skillet to medium-high, and boil until the liquid is reduced to about half its original volume, 6 to 8 minutes. Skim occasionally to remove as much of the scum and fat as possible.

While the cooking liquid is reducing, prepare the roux for the sauce. Melt the butter in a saucepan over medium-low heat. When hot, stir in the flour and simmer for 3 to 4 minutes, stirring occasionally. This is to remove the starchy taste of the raw flour. Place the saucepan in the refrigerator or freezer to cool while you strain the reducing liquid. Cooling the roux will prevent the sauce from lumping when the reduced cooking liquid is added.

Strain the reduced cooking liquid through a sieve lined with cheesecloth or a kitchen towel. You should have about 2 cups.

Rinse the skillet and wipe the inside dry. Return the chicken to the skillet, cover, and set aside.

Place the saucepan with the roux over medium heat. Stir in the reduced liquid and bring to a full boil, stirring occasionally. When the sauce reaches a full boil, it will be completely thickened.

Beat the egg yolks and cream together in a mixing bowl until well combined and no streaks of yellow appear in the cream. Slowly pour about half the sauce into the egg and cream mixture, beating constantly. This is to gradually warm the eggs and prevent them from curdling. Reverse the process, and beat the egg yolk and cream mixture into the saucepan. Place over medium heat and bring to a boil, stirring frequently. Add the lemon juice, any juices that may have accumulated on the plate under the chicken (why waste all that good flavor?), and season with salt and pepper to taste.

FINAL HEATING: Pour the sauce over the chicken in the skillet. Place over medium-low heat, cover, and simmer for 5 minutes to reheat the chicken.

To serve, arrange the chicken and sauce in a decorative bowl or serving dish, and sprinkle with chopped parsley. This fricassee, which is utterly simple and honest in flavor, is delicious with rice (I think it is even better with boiled potatoes), and a crusty, homemade bread.

I've known red-wine fiends who would be more than comfortable serving any number of red wines with a chicken fricassee, but I feel that the bird's "soft" flavors, coupled with a "soft" white sauce, should have a wine with the same softness and depth of flavor. Something like a Johannisberg Riesling, Grey Riesling, or Chénin Blanc—all from California—would be ideal.

To add more flavor and textural variation to the basic fricassee, any number of ingredients can be cooked and added to the sauce just before the dish is reheated. A number of variations are suggested below.

One of the great advantages of a chicken fricassee is that it can be prepared several hours or even a day ahead, and refrigerated until needed. The only difference is that it will take 10 to 15 minutes to reheat, rather than 5, and the chicken should be turned once or twice during the reheating.

CHICKEN FRICASSEE
WITH TARRAGON

❖❖❖

A simple and great way to vary the basic idea of a white fricassee is to flavor it with fresh herbs. Tarragon is my favorite.

Prepare the basic white fricassee as directed in the master recipe (above), adding 1 tablespoon of crushed dried tarragon to the stock and white wine before bringing it to a boil. Just before pouring the sauce over the chicken for reheating, strain and stir in 2 tablespoons of chopped fresh tarragon and 1 tablespoon each of chopped parsley and chives, if available.

Serve with the same wine and vegetables suggested in the master recipe.

CHICKEN FRICASSEE WITH MUSHROOMS AND ONIONS

———— ❖❖❖ ————

This garnish of mushrooms and onions keeps true to the color coordination of a strictly white fricassee. The tastes are also flattering to the chicken, and they add both visual and textural interest to the recipe.

12 *to* 16 *pearl onions*   3 *Tablespoons butter*
¼ *pound mushrooms* (125
   grams)

Carefully trim the root end of the onions, leaving as much of the root as possible attached to the onion. Peel the onions. Drop into boiling water, reduce the heat, and simmer until tender. Set aside.

If the mushrooms are large, trim the bottoms of the stems and quarter them. If small button mushrooms are available, trim the stems, leave them whole. Melt the butter in a skillet over medium heat. When hot, add the mushrooms and sauté for 1 to 2 minutes. Set aside.

Prepare a white chicken fricassee as directed in the master recipe (see page 74). Just before pouring the sauce over the chicken for the final reheating, stir in the mushrooms and onions.

Serve with the same wine and vegetables suggested in the master recipe.

CHICKEN FRICASSEE
WITH MUSSELS

—————— ❖❖❖ ——————

Mussels and chicken complement each other beautifully, though they are only rarely seen together. It is a lovely and festive marriage, and one I am particularly fond of.

Carefully scrub clean a pint of mussels, removing as much of the beard as possible. Prepare a basic white fricassee as directed in the master recipe (see page 74). After the boiling stock and wine is poured over the chicken, toss the mussels into the skillet on top of the chicken, then cover the skillet and simmer. After 6 to 8 minutes, the mussels will be opened and cooked. Remove the mussels with a slotted spoon, and continue with the recipe as directed.

Any mussels which have not opened should be discarded.

The mussels can be removed from their shells, if you wish, and added to the final sauce before reheating the chicken. I prefer to leave them in their shells, which looks more decorative, and simply arrange them around the chicken for the reheating.

Serve with parsleyed potatoes and a good, dry white Burgundy, or perhaps a dry, full-bodied Italian white wine such as Orvieto Secco.

Crayfish or shrimp can be substituted for the mussels.

COQ AU VIN ROUGE

—————— ❖❖❖ ——————

Coq au Vin usually means Coq au Vin Rouge; a brown chicken fricassee cooked in red wine. It can be a beautiful dish—with an exciting variety of textures and tastes in the garnish, and a lovely, rich chicken-flavored red-wine sauce.

The "Coq" in Coq au Vin indicates that originally this dish was prepared with a farmyard cock, probably about a year old. The red wine, by orthodoxy and origin, should be a red Burgundy, though I suspect you will use a better red wine than most cocks in Burgundy ever hoped they would simmer in. Also by tradition, the final sauce was thickened with fresh chicken or pork blood. As I am occasionally wont to do, I set about developing this recipe by adhering to all the traditions. I used a cock which was close to a year old (and which it took my poulterer a week and a half to obtain for me), a good but not great red Burgundy, and I thickened the sauce with fresh pork blood. To tell the truth, I could not eat it and left the table nauseated. Let me tell you why. Using the cock, and therefore simmering it for 2½ hours, gave the red wine an incredibly rich body and chicken flavor. So far so good. The good red Burgundy was perfect, if a bit expensive. But the blood is what got to me —it left the sauce thick and beautifully shiny, but gave it a bloody, iron taste that I could not get down my throat. So purists be damned, I prefer flour!

This is a good example of a brown fricassee. It differs from a white fricassee in two basic respects: the chicken is browned during the initial sautéing, and the final sauce is red-wine brown. The theories and principles, however, remain unchanged and are detailed in the master recipe (see page 74).

To our Coq au Vin, then:

½ *cup flour*
1½ *teaspoons salt*
½ *teaspoon freshly ground black pepper*
1 *3½- to 4-pound chicken, cut into serving pieces (see page 224)* (1½–1¾ *kilograms*)
2 *Tablespoons butter*
2 *Tablespoons oil*
¼ *cup Cognac*
4 *Tablespoons butter*
1 *medium onion, chopped*

2 *carrots, chopped*
1 *celery rib, chopped*
2 *garlic cloves, finely chopped*
1 *bottle of a good red Burgundy (reserve ½ cup for the garnish)*
1 *bay leaf, crumbled*
½ *teaspoon thyme*
1 *cup Basic Brown Sauce (see page 216) or 1 cup brown beef stock*

THE GARNISH

2 *Tablespoons butter or oil*
3 *to 4 ounces salt pork, finely diced* (75–100 *grams*)

12 *to 16 pearl onions, peeled*
12 *to 16 small mushroom caps*

TO THICKEN THE SAUCE

3 *Tablespoons flour, kneaded*	*Salt*
into	*Freshly ground black pepper*
3 *Tablespoons butter*	

Combine the flour, salt and pepper in a bowl, and mix well. Roll the chicken pieces in the seasoned flour so that they are evenly and lightly coated. Shake off any excess flour. Flouring the chicken will help with the browning and will also act as a slight thickening for the sauce.

Melt the butter and oil over medium heat in a straight-sided skillet large enough to hold all the chicken in one layer. When hot, add the chicken, skin side down. Sauté for 8 to 10 minutes, turning occasionally, until the chicken is nicely browned on all sides. Transfer the chicken to a plate. Pour the Cognac into the skillet, and working quickly, scrape all of the brown-encrusted bits on the bottom of the pan into the rapidly evaporating Cognac. Pour the deglazing juices into a saucepan, and set aside.

Add the butter to the skillet, and place over medium-low heat. When hot, add the onion, carrots, celery, and garlic. Sauté the vegetables until tender but not browned, about 6 minutes, stirring occasionally. Transfer the vegetables to the saucepan with the deglazing juices. Rinse the skillet and wipe dry. Arrange the chicken in the skillet, skin side up. Pour any of the juices that accumulated on the plate under the chicken into the saucepan.

Pour the red wine into the saucepan with the vegetables, remembering to reserve ½ cup for the garnish. Add the brown sauce or stock, the bay leaf, and thyme. Bring to a boil over medium-high heat.

Pour the boiling liquid and sautéed vegetables over the chicken, and place over medium-high heat. As soon as the liquid comes back to a boil, reduce the heat to low, and simmer for 25 to 30 minutes.

While the chicken is simmering, prepare the garnish. Place the butter or oil in a skillet over medium heat. When hot, add the diced salt pork, and sauté, stirring often, until the pork is golden brown and rendered of all its fat. With a slotted spoon, transfer to absorbent paper to drain.

Add the onions to the skillet with the rendered fat from the salt pork. Sauté the onions for 6 to 8 minutes, shaking the pan back and forth every couple of minutes. The onions should be only lightly browned. Drain off any excess fat. Add the red wine and the mushroom caps to the skillet. Cover, reduce the heat, and simmer until the mushrooms and onions feel tender when pierced with a toothpick or skewer, about 10 minutes. Remove from the heat and set aside.

When the chicken has simmered for 25 to 30 minutes, test for doneness (see page 76). When the white meat test's done, transfer it to a plate and cover it with a piece of aluminum foil. Transfer the dark meat when it's done to the plate with the white meat.

Increase the heat under the skillet to medium-high. Boil until the cooking liquid is reduced by half, about 8 to 10 minutes. Strain the sauce into a clean saucepan, and skim off any fat or scum that has risen to the surface. There should be about 2 cups. Place the saucepan over medium heat; gradually beat in the kneaded butter and flour until the sauce is thick enough to slightly coat the back of a spoon. It will probably take most of the butter and flour suggested. Taste the sauce, and season with salt and pepper.

Rinse the skillet and wipe dry. Arrange the chicken back in the skillet. Surround with garnish: the salt pork, onions, and mushrooms. Pour in the sauce and place over medium heat. When the sauce begins to bubble, reduce the heat to low, cover, and simmer until the chicken is thoroughly heated, about 5 minutes. Serve at once with parsleyed potatoes.

This dish is produced world-wide, certainly wherever there are vineyards, but because so much of its loveliness lies in its origins, I would prefer to be traditional and serve it with a Burgundy such as Gevrey-Chambertin, Mercurey, the less expensive Nuits-Saint-Georges, or a Burgundy-style Pinot Noir from California. Traditionally, Coq au Vin is not served with a great or expensive wine; however, if you want to splurge, one of the greats of Burgundy such as Romanée-Conti, La Tâche, Richebourg, or Grandes Échezeaux would be gorgeous.

Makes 6 to 8 servings.

COUNTRY CAPTAIN

———— ❖❖❖ ————

This is an Anglo-Indian dish which sailed across the Atlantic in the middle of the nineteenth century. "Country Captain" was a term applied by the British to a captain of the Sepoys, native Indians trained as soldiers and paid by the British.

4 *Tablespoons butter*
1 *small onion, finely chopped*
1 *small carrot, finely chopped*
½ *small green pepper, finely chopped*
2 *garlic cloves, finely chopped*
2 *Tablespoons oil*
½ *cup flour*
1½ *teaspoons salt*
1 *teaspoon freshly ground black pepper*
1 2½- *to 3-pound chicken, cut into serving pieces* (1¼–1½ *kilograms*)

1 *can (about ¾ pound) peeled Italian plum tomatoes* (about 350 grams)
2 *cups chicken stock*
2 *Tablespoons curry powder*
¼ *cup desiccated coconut* (*unsweetened, shredded coconut*)
¼ *cup sultana raisins*
Salt
Freshly ground black pepper
Slivered, toasted almonds and chopped parsley for garnish

Melt the butter over medium-low heat in a straight-sided skillet large enough to hold all the chicken in one layer. When hot, add the onion, carrot, green pepper, and garlic, and sauté until tender but not browned, about 6 minutes, stirring occasionally. Transfer the vegetables to a saucepan. Add the oil to the skillet.

Combine the flour, salt and pepper in a bowl. Roll the chicken pieces in the seasoned flour, patting off any excess. Arrange the chicken in the skillet, skin side down, and sauté for 6 to 8 minutes, turning occasionally, until the chicken is nicely browned on all sides.

While the chicken is sautéing, add the can of tomatoes, the stock, and the curry powder to the saucepan with the sautéed vegetables. Bring to a boil over medium-high heat.

When the chicken has finished sautéing, pour the boiling sauce over it. Cover, reduce the heat to low, and simmer for 15 minutes. Stir in the coconut and sultanas, and simmer 5 minutes longer.

Test the chicken for doneness (see page 76), arranging the white meat on a heated platter when it finishes cooking. When the dark meat is done, return the white meat to the skillet and simmer for a minute or two to reheat. Taste the sauce, and season with salt and pepper.

Arrange the Country Captain in a decorative serving bowl, and garnish with toasted almond slivers and chopped parsley. Serve immediately, accompanied by boiled rice.

Many will prefer beer with this dish. Some may even prefer a red wine. My choice would be a full-bodied white wine with an extravagant bouquet such as a Riesling or the fuller, "spicier" Gewürztraminer from France's Alsace region. The English would certainly have approved of this wine with a Country Captain.

BASIC CHICKEN STEW

❖❖❖

MASTER RECIPE

❖

Stewing a fowl really means poaching it—only it takes longer —since the moist heat must thoroughly penetrate the chicken and break down the tough fibers of the meat.

1 4½- to 5-pound fowl, cut into serving pieces (see page 224) (2–2¼ kilograms)
2 medium onions, sliced
4 to 5 carrots, sliced
3 to 4 celery ribs, sliced
2 garlic cloves, unpeeled and smashed with the side of a cook's knife

1 bay leaf, crumbled
1 teaspoon dried thyme
2 teaspoons salt
1 teaspoon freshly ground black pepper
Chicken stock

Remove any excess fat from the chicken. Arrange the chicken in a very large pot, and add the remaining ingredients. Add enough boiling stock to come 2 to 3 inches above the chicken. Place over medium-high heat, partially covered, and bring back to a boil. Reduce the heat and simmer until the chicken is tender, anywhere from 2 hours to 3 hours, depending on the age and toughness of the chicken. The chicken should feel tender when poked with a fork, but should not be cooked until it falls off the bones.

Every 20 to 30 minutes, skim the poaching liquid to remove the scum and fat that have risen to the surface.

Arrange the chicken on a warm platter or heated plates. Strain the broth and season with additional salt and pepper. Stewed chicken is flavorful enough to serve as the French do, with a little of the poaching liquid spooned over it, though I prefer it with a white sauce made from some of the broth and a little milk or cream (see page 203). This dish is good with a great variety of vegetables: rice or noodles, boiled potatoes, onions, carrots, or brussels sprouts. Serve with a simple red wine such as a light-bodied but pleasing Cabernet or Merlot, produced in Italy's northern wine-growing region of Friuli Venezia Giulia, or with a Valpolicella, produced in Italy's Veronese vineyards.

STEWED CHICKEN WITH PARSLEY DUMPLINGS

❖❖❖

This is a wonderful combination of textures and complementary flavors, and very much the kind of simple, honest food one would have hoped to find in a farmhouse kitchen at the turn of the century.

Add ½ cup finely chopped fresh parsley to the dumplings (see page 194); drop dumplings into the stew 30 minutes before the fowl is done. If the chicken is not tender when the dumplings have cooked for 30 minutes, remove them; then return them to the pot to reheat for 4 or 5 minutes when the chicken is tender enough to serve.

To serve, arrange a piece of the fowl and 2 or 3 dumplings in a large soup bowl. Ladle in some of the broth, sprinkle with additional chopped parsley, if you wish, and serve immediately.

This dish doesn't call for a very big or complex red wine. In fact, its flavors would be overcome by such a wine. Instead I'd suggest one of the lighter-bodied Petit Sirahs from California, a California Gamay Beaujolais, or an extremely light Beaujolais from France.

···❖ 4 ❖···

SAUTÉING AND FRYING

———— ❖❖❖ ————

As I melted the butter in the pan,
added the eggs, shook the pan, and swirled
the omelet around I suddenly realized something
I had never considered before—an omelet
is a sauté of eggs!

JAMES BEARD,
*James Beard's Theory & Practice
of Good Cooking*

No cooking technique is used so often and with so many different foods as the sauté. Whether in its own right, or as part of another cooking procedure, hardly a day goes by when the experienced cook doesn't sauté something: beef, veal, pork, rabbit, or quail; a whole legion of vegetables, even lettuce; fruits for a dessert, or almonds to top a fillet of sole. Yet when it comes to chicken, the whole category of sautés has been virtually ignored by Americans.

The word *sauté* means jumped; and while chicken isn't jumped around the pan as, say, mushrooms would be, the chicken is jumped in the sense that it is turned often to ensure even coloring and cooking.

Throughout this chapter the sautés are prepared by sautéing the chicken for about 8 minutes, then covering the skillet and "finishing it off" in the oven. This is by no means the only way to sauté, but it's the one I've found is best. There are two kinds of chicken sauté, white and brown. In a white sauté, the chicken develops only the faintest sign of coloring and the exposed flesh becomes white and plump. A brown sauté is cooked over higher heat and the chicken turns a rich, golden-brown color. Traditionally the white sauté is used when the dish calls for a white sauce, and the brown sauté when a darker sauce is used. The master recipe for a simple chicken sauté gives directions for both kinds of sauté. For any given recipe, the choice is a matter of personal preference. Even where I have indicated my preference—in the chicken sauté with cream, for example—if you would rather have a rich, golden-brown skin, then by all means sauté the chicken brown. Or, if you notice that the heat is too high and your white sauté is browning the chicken, raise the heat and do a complete brown sauté.

The great variety of chicken sautés comes not so much from varying the basic preparation as from the garniture and sauce preparation. The recipes in this chapter only begin to touch on the vast number of taste combinations possible. There's a master recipe for the simplest and most basic chicken sauté, followed by some interesting and exciting variations in the garniture. The idea for one of the garnishes, a hearty taste combination of tomato wedges and black olives brought to life with freshly grated lemon zest and a julienne of leeks, came from a dish I ate at the 107th-floor restaurant of New York's World Trade Center.

But even without paying any particular attention to the garnish, the possibilities for different sautés are almost infinite. For the sauce can be finished by simply adding about half a cup of any sauce you have on hand to the skillet juices with a little stock, and then reducing it slightly. Any of the sauces listed on pages 202 to 205 can be used.

In a chicken sauté, sealing is not just an important principle but, as in grilling and broiling, it is the *only* principle. The sealing process begins as soon as the pieces of chicken added to the skillet are filmed in hot butter, or butter and oil. Before adding the chicken, pat it thoroughly dry with absorbent paper or a clean kitchen towel. Excess moisture on the surface of the chicken turns to steam when it comes in contact with the hot fat and steams the chicken, rather than allowing the meat to seal. It also makes it difficult for the chicken to brown evenly. When you add the chicken, don't overcrowd the skillet. The chicken needs breathing space, and no two pieces should be touching. It is also easier to turn the chicken in an uncrowded pan, and the extra few minutes spent sautéing the chicken in two or even three batches is well worth the effort.

The best pans for sautéing chicken have heavy bottoms, clad in either aluminum or copper, straight sides about 3 inches high, and tight-fitting covers. Mine are all made of stainless steel and have short handles on either side of the pan. A pan with a long, heavy handle on one side is more traditional but unfortunately won't fit into my small oven. The only other piece of equipment you need for a chicken sauté is a pair of tongs. Having worked so hard to seal the chicken properly, don't break that seal by jabbing the chicken with a fork every time it is turned. Tongs also make it easier to hold and turn the chicken. A pair of kitchen chop sticks—the very long ones that are connected by a string at one end—are excellent for turning sautéed or fried foods, if you are comfortable using them.

The difference between sautéing and frying is in the amount of oil or fat used. A sauté is a dish in which the food has been cooked in hot oil or fat that just films the bottom of a pan. Frying, on the other hand, is done in about 2 inches of fat or oil, virtually submerging the food in what might be called a "surprise attack."

Today we casually think of frying chicken with a sense of delight and excitement, the dark outside coating of crumbs or flour that crisply seals in all the rich, juicy flavor of the chicken. But frying wasn't always so popular. Mrs. Bradley, in *The British Housewife* (c. 1770), had this to say about it:

> After broiling we are to mention frying, though little need be said about it. It is a coarse and greasy Kind of Cookery, in Fashion in the Country, where there are great Appetites and strong Stomachs, but it is at present entirely left off in genteel Families. . . .

Brillat-Savarin, the early-nineteenth-century French writer whose book, *The Physiology of Taste*, is perhaps the most famous book ever written about food, was far kinder:

> The whole secret of good frying comes from the *surprise;* for such is called the action of the boiling liquid which chars and browns, at the very instant of immersion, the outside surfaces of whatever is being fried.
>
> By means of this *surprise,* a kind of glove is formed, which contains the body of food, keeps the grease from penetrating, and concentrates the inner juices, which themselves undergo an interior cooking which gives to the food all the flavor it is capable of producing.

For this "surprise attack" the oil or fat must be the right temperature. I find 350° F. best for chicken. Be certain that the oil is fully preheated before adding the chicken. On an electric frying pan there is usually an indicator light; if you are frying on top of the range in a deep pan with a frying basket, mount a candy or deep-frying thermometer on the side of the pot and check often to see that the temperature is evenly maintained at 350° F. There should always be a generous amount of oil for frying because the chicken must be virtually submerged in it to seal and cook properly, and the temperature shouldn't be lowered drastically when the food is added.

If the oil or fat is clean (the first time it is being used), the first batch of chicken fried in it will not color as deeply as successive batches, but as you continue to fry, the oil will become darker and the chicken browner. Frying oil can be strained, placed in a tightly covered jar, and reused a second or perhaps even a third time. But label the jar as to what was cooked in the oil, for there is nothing more unappealing than fishy-tasting chicken, or chickeny-tasting vegetables. Although I usually use peanut oil, almost any bland oil can be used for frying.

As a general rule I use a deep electric frying pan with a wire rack on the bottom. Using a rack or deep-frying basket is very important. If the chicken is allowed to sit on the bottom of the frying pan, it will cook from the heat of the pan, often burning in spots, rather than from the heat of the fat. I don't like frying on top of the range because of the need to repeatedly adjust the heat so that the temperature of the oil remains constant.

There are certainly as many recipes for Southern fried chicken as there are Southerners, and there is no agreement on anything, except that it should be fried. Some Southerners insist that the only way to fry chicken is in bacon fat; others are equally vehement in their belief in lard, or lard and butter; while still others concede to peanut oil or vegetable shortening. Then there are the schools which say that chicken should be dipped in eggs before being breaded; or in milk or buttermilk only, no eggs; or in a combination of milk and eggs; and those that claim it shouldn't be dipped at all. There is even disagreement about the breading: often it is white flour seasoned with salt and pepper, with a touch of cayenne or cinnamon added, but sometimes it is whole-wheat flour or cracker crumbs. And not everyone believes in seasoning the flour, so even when to salt and pepper the chicken is up for debate. Then there are those who believe in batter dipping; and the "moderns" who roll their chicken in crushed cornflakes or Rice Krispies. Fortunately, there are only two schools to tell us how to bread the chicken: one insists it be shaken in a "sack," the other rolled on a plate. And on and on it goes.

Our heads now spinning from the search for the *real* Southern fried chicken, we turn to James Beard, who shatters us completely by saying that "Although everyone thinks fried chicken is as American as blueberry pie, it did not originate here." We have, however, as Mr. Beard points out, adopted it—perhaps from the Viennese *Wiener Backhendl*, and made it American.

Regardless of how one cooks fried chicken, properly done, it has few rivals!

SIMPLE CHICKEN SAUTÉ

MASTER RECIPE

Simple and fast to prepare, sautéing is a great way to prepare chicken. Every piece is rich, juicy, and full of flavor. The total cooking time is about half an hour, and while the chicken is in the oven the vegetables can be prepared. Or it can be made ahead and gently warmed in its sauce.

This recipe includes directions for both a white and brown sauté. For an explanation of the differences, see page 94.

1 2½- to 3-pound chicken, cut into serving pieces (see page 224) (1¼–1½ kilograms) *Freshly ground black pepper* *Salt*	3 Tablespoons butter, or 2 Tablespoons oil and 1 Tablespoon butter

THE SAUCE

½ cup chicken stock 2 Tablespoons butter (optional)	Salt Freshly ground black pepper

Preheat oven to 375° F.

Dry the chicken thoroughly. This ensures proper browning and searing when the chicken is sautéed. Season with salt and pepper.

A WHITE CHICKEN SAUTÉ: In a heavy skillet (with a tight-fitting cover) large enough to hold all the chicken in a single layer, melt the butter over medium-low heat. When hot, add the white meat (the wings and breasts), skin side down, and sauté for 8 to 10 minutes, turning frequently. The chicken should be watched carefully and turned as soon as the exposed flesh turns white or opaque and begins to plump. Regulate the heat so that the chicken develops a light, golden hue but never browns. The wings will be easier to cook if the tips have been removed at the first joint, and the breasts will cook more evenly if the upper ridge of the breastbone has been removed. When turning the chicken, use tongs, not a fork that pierces the meat.

Place the wings and breasts on a plate and sauté the pieces of dark meat. When sautéing the second batch, it may be necessary to reduce the heat to prevent browning. If the butter has begun to burn, immediately remove the chicken, pour off the burned fat, wipe the skillet, and add 3 tablespoons of fresh butter.

A BROWN CHICKEN SAUTÉ: Follow the method above for a white chicken sauté, except cook the chicken over medium heat until it is an even golden brown.

INITIAL BAKING: Cover the skillet, which contains the dark meat only, and place in a preheated 375° F. oven for 8 minutes.

FINAL BAKING: For the final baking, add the white meat to the skillet, cover, and place back in the oven for another 12 to 15 minutes. Test for doneness.

To TEST FOR DONENESS: Insert an instantly registering thermometer into the thickest part of the meat without touching the bone. Dark meat should register 165° F., white meat only 140° F.

When done, arrange chicken on a heated platter, drape loosely in foil to keep warm, and prepare the sauce.

THE SAUCE: Place the skillet over medium-high heat and stir in the stock. Reduce for a minute or two to about two thirds its original volume, scraping the brown-encrusted bits on the bottom of the skillet into the sauce. Remove from the heat and enrich, if you wish, by swirling in the butter. Taste and season with salt and pepper. Pour over chicken and serve immediately.

Buttered green beans, broccoli, peas, or Brussels sprouts go well with sautéed chicken, adding both color and texture to the plate. Serve with a hearty, medium-bodied red wine, perhaps a Côtes du Rhône or a California Zinfandel.

Makes 4 to 6 servings.

CHICKEN SAUTÉ WITH CREAM

———— ❖❖❖ ————

Prepare a white chicken sauté as directed in the master recipe (see page 93). When chicken has completed its final baking, arrange on a heated platter.

2 *Tablespoons butter*	½ *cup heavy cream*
1 *Tablespoon finely chopped*	*Salt*
shallots	*Freshly ground black pepper*

Pour all the juices from the skillet, and reserve. Melt the butter in the skillet over medium-low heat. Add the shallots, and sauté until tender, about 3 minutes, scraping up any encrusted bits on the bottom of the skillet as the shallots are stirred. Add the reserved juices and cream. Raise heat to medium-high and stir vigorously while reducing for a minute or two to about two thirds its original volume. Season with salt and pepper to taste. Pour over chicken and serve immediately.

Serve with parsleyed potatoes and buttered broccoli, and a crisp, dry white wine such as a Mâcon Blanc or a Muscadet.

Makes 4 to 6 servings.

If you sauté 2 or 3 finely chopped garlic cloves with the shallots, you will have Chicken Sauté with Garlic Cream. Likewise, if you add ½ cup dry white wine, you'll have Chicken Sauté with White Wine Cream Sauce.

Once you have become familiar with the basic technique, it is a good idea to look around the kitchen before you begin cooking—a little white wine left over from yesterday's dinner might not be called for in the recipe, but could well improve its flavor.

CHICKEN SAUTÉ WITH WHOLE GARLIC CLOVES

❖❖❖

And scorne not Garlicke like some that thinke
It only makes men winke, and drinke, and stinke

ENGLISH PROVERB

This is a garlic lover's delight. A whole *head* of garlic is used to flavor the sauce and then becomes part of the garnish. But don't shriek in horror at the thought—even if you're not a garlic fanatic, you'll love this dish. The garlic is peeled and simmered in water first, making it surprisingly tender and delicate, both in texture and taste.

Prepare a brown chicken sauté and complete the initial baking as directed in the master recipe (see page 93).

1 *whole head garlic*	*½ cup chicken stock*
1 *teaspoon chopped fresh*	*Salt*
rosemary or ¼ teaspoon	*Freshly ground black pepper*
crushed *dried rosemary*	*Chopped parsley for garnish*
¼ cup dry white wine	

Break a *whole head* of garlic into cloves and peel. Place the garlic in boiling water, reduce heat, and simmer for 25 to 30 minutes, until tender. Drain, being careful not to mash the garlic cloves. When adding the white meat to the skillet for the final baking, add the garlic cloves, rosemary, and wine. Cover, and replace the skillet in the oven for the final baking of 12 to 15 minutes. When done (see page 94), arrange the chicken on a heated platter. Spoon the garlic cloves onto a plate, and reserve.

Place the skillet over medium-high heat. Add the stock and reduce for a minute or two to about half its original volume, stirring and scraping the brown-encrusted bits on the bottom of the skillet into the sauce. Season with salt and pepper to taste. Reduce heat to low, add the garlic cloves, and simmer gently for a minute or so to warm the garlic and blend the final tastes together. Pour over the chicken, sprinkle with chopped parsley, and serve immediately.

I like to serve this with a crusty homemade bread (which can be spread with a garlic clove or two), or a salad with a vinaigrette dressing, and perhaps some boiled potatoes. To stand up to the garlic, one of the very fruity but dry-finishing and elegant wines of the Rheingau in Germany, from the vineyards of Eltville, Rauenthal or Hattenheim, would be ideal. However, as these are sometimes difficult to find, an Orvieto Secco from Italy would be an excellent and less expensive alternative.

Makes 4 to 6 servings.

CHICKEN SAUTÉ
WITH TARRAGON

——— ❖❖❖ ———

Sauté the chicken brown and complete the initial baking as directed in the master recipe (see page 93).

2 *to* 3 *Tablespoons chopped fresh tarragon, or* 2 *teaspoons crushed dried tarragon*	*Salt*
	Freshly ground black pepper
	Additional fresh tarragon or chopped parsley for garnish
1 *teaspoon lemon juice*	
½ *cup chicken stock*	

Remove the dark meat from the skillet and stir in the tarragon and lemon juice. Return all the chicken to the skillet, turning each piece in the herbed juices as it is added. Cover, and set back in the oven for the final baking of 12 to 15 minutes. When chicken is done (see page 94), arrange on a heated platter and drape loosely in foil.

Place the skillet over medium-high heat. Add the stock and reduce for a minute or two to about half its original volume, stirring and scraping the brown-encrusted bits on the bottom of the skillet into the sauce. Season with salt and pepper to taste. Pour over the chicken, sprinkle with additional fresh tarragon or chopped parsley, and serve immediately.

Accompany with sautéed mushrooms, broccoli, or glazed onions or carrots, and a somewhat unusual but very pleasing dry white wine from Italy's Umbrian Hills such as Est Est Est.

Makes 4 to 6 servings.

Tarragon is by no means the only herb you could use in this recipe. There are so many herbs and combinations of herbs that go well with chicken—rosemary, thyme, lemon thyme, basil, chives, parsley, marjoram, and chervil. Substitute 3 to 4 tablespoons of any herb, or combination of herbs, or 2 to 3 teaspoons of crushed dried herbs for the tarragon, and create your own herbed chicken sauté. If you would like the herbs in a cream sauce, add ½ cup heavy cream to the skillet with the stock.

Herbs sometimes look dead after they have been cooked in a recipe, and it is often a good idea to strain the sauce, and then stir in fresh herbs just before sending the dish to the table.

CHICKEN SAUTÉ
JAMES BEARD

———— ❖❖❖ ————

I first tasted this garnish as Rack of Lamb James Beard at the magnificent 107th-floor restaurant on the top of New York's World Trade Center. And I wondered for several days whether my excitement was really about the beautiful combination of tomatoes, black olives, leeks, and lemon zest, or if it was not about the view of Manhattan from a quarter mile high. I think it was a bit of both, but the garnish is just as good at sea level!

Grated zest of ½ large lemon
1 *small leek, white part only,*
very thinly sliced and
separated into rings
3 *small tomatoes, cut in*
wedges
10 *to* 12 *black olives, prefer-*
ably the small Italian ones
with the jet-black, wrinkled
skins, or Nice olives

½ *cup chicken stock*
Salt
Freshly ground black pepper
Chopped parsley

Sauté the chicken brown and complete the initial baking as directed in the master recipe (page 93).

When the initial baking is completed, remove all the chicken from the skillet and set aside. Stir the lemon zest and leeks into the pan juices. Place over low heat, and simmer for 3 or 4 minutes. Add the tomato wedges and olives, cover, and simmer gently until the tomatoes are warmed through. With a slotted spoon, carefully remove the contents of the skillet. Place all the chicken back in the skillet, both the white and dark meat, and arrange the vegetables on top. Cover, and return to the oven for the final baking of 12 to 15 minutes. When done (see page 94), arrange the chicken and garnish on a heated platter, and drape loosely in foil.

Place the skillet over medium-high heat. Add the stock and reduce for a minute or two to about half its original volume, stirring and scraping the brown-encrusted bits on the bottom of the skillet into the sauce. Season with salt and pepper to taste. Pour over the chicken, and garnish with chopped parsley. Serve immediately.

Serve with rice or shoestring potatoes, and chopped spinach flavored with nutmeg. Since this dish is so reminiscent of Provençal cooking, I would recommend a not very full-bodied red wine from the Provence vineyards, which nestle just above France's glorious Riviera. Something like a Bandol, Palette, or Bellet would be nice. A red Bordeaux Supérieure would be a good alternative.

Makes 4 to 6 servings.

If you like anchovies, add 4 or 5 anchovy fillets, coarsely chopped, and 1 tablespoon capers to the skillet when simmering the lemon zest and leeks. Be careful not to oversalt the sauce.

CHICKEN WITH
SAUTÉED PINEAPPLE

❖❖❖

If you are not accustomed to sautéed fruit—apples, bananas, pineapples, or whatever—I think you will find this an exciting new taste sensation. The pineapple develops a buttery richness and a caramelized golden-brown color as it is gently sautéed.

Prepare a brown chicken sauté as directed in the master recipe (see page 93). While the chicken is baking, sauté the pineapple.

1 *small ripe pineapple, peeled and cored*	½ *cup chicken stock*
	Salt
6 *Tablespoons* unsalted *butter*	*Freshly ground black pepper*

Slice the pineapple into rings about ¼ inch thick. Melt the butter in a large skillet over medium-low heat. When hot, add the pineapple slices, 3 or 4 at a time, and sauté until tender and lightly colored, turning occasionally. Depending on the ripeness of the pineapple and the thickness of the slices, this will take 6 to 10 minutes. It may be necessary to reduce the heat during the cooking to prevent the butter from burning.

When the chicken has finished its final baking, arrange on a heated platter and surround with the pineapple. Drape loosely in foil.

Mix the stock with the juices in the skillet and place over medium-high heat. Reduce for a minute or two to about half its original volume, stirring and scraping the brown-encrusted bits on the bottom of the skillet into the sauce. Season to taste with salt and pepper. Spoon over the chicken and pineapple, and serve immediately.

Serve with rice cooked in chicken stock, and accompany with either a Moselle from Germany or an Entre-Deux-Mers from Bordeaux. The former will be fruity and very light and elegant, with a slight sweet finish; the latter will be fuller-bodied and slightly sweeter on the finish.

Makes 4 to 6 servings.

CHICKEN SAUTÉ WITH CHESTNUTS, ONIONS, AND MUSHROOMS

For me, chestnuts have always heralded the approach of winter. When the first smells of roasting chestnuts came from the street vendors along Fifth Avenue, winter was here and the windows would soon be decorated for Christmas. I can only think of this as a winter dish, though it can be made year round if you use canned chestnuts.

Prepare the garnish. This can be done ahead of time, if you wish.

½ pound fresh chestnuts (250 grams)	*1 cup Basic Brown Sauce* (see page 216)
12 to 14 small pearl onions	*¼ cup red wine*
3 Tablespoons butter	*Salt*
¼ pound small mushrooms, stems removed (125 grams)	*Freshly ground black pepper* *Chopped parsley*

With a sharp, pointed knife, pierce through the shell of the chestnuts and cut completely around the narrow edge, beginning at the point, running down through the base and back up to the point. Place the chestnuts in a saucepan with cold water. Bring to a boil over medium heat, and boil for 2 minutes. Cool the chestnuts under running cold water. Squeeze the cut edge of the chestnuts between your index finger and thumb. Out pops the chestnut, clear of shell and inner skin!

When all the chestnuts have been peeled, place them in boiling salted water, reduce the heat and simmer until tender, about 20 minutes.

While the chestnuts are simmering, prepare the onions. Peel the onions, cutting off as little of the root end as possible. If too much of the root end is removed, the onions will fall apart when cooked. Place the onions in boiling water, reduce the heat and simmer until tender. Drain, and cool under cold running water.

Melt the butter over medium heat. When hot, add the mushrooms and sauté for 2 to 3 minutes. Remove and set aside.

Now sauté the chicken brown and complete the final baking as directed in the master recipe (see page 93). When done, arrange the chicken on a heated platter, and prepare the sauce. Place the skillet with its pan juices over medium-high heat. Add the brown sauce and red wine. Stir, scraping the brown-encrusted bits on the bottom of the skillet into the sauce, and reduce for a minute or two to thicken slightly. Add the chestnuts, onions, and mushrooms to the sauce, cover, reduce heat, and simmer until the garnish is hot. Season with salt and pepper to taste. Spoon the garnish around the platter, pour some sauce over the chicken, sprinkle with chopped parsley, and serve immediately.

This winter meal needs little more than sautéed potatoes and perhaps a Côtes du Rhône or a Corbières, which are extremely robust red wines, perfect for winter.

Makes 4 to 6 servings.

CHICKEN SAUTÉ WITH MUSHROOMS AND ARTICHOKE BOTTOMS

❖❖❖

This marriage of the sweet taste of the artichoke bottoms with the softness of fresh tarragon and the quiet flavor of the mushrooms is one of the most beautiful in this book. The recipe calls for canned or frozen artichoke bottoms. If you prepare your own by poaching and trimming 4 or 5 large, fresh artichokes, the taste and texture will be even better.

Sauté chicken white and place in the oven for the initial baking as directed in the master recipe (page 93).

4 *Tablespoons butter*
½ *pound small mushrooms,*
   quartered (250 grams)
12 *ounces (approximately)*
   canned or frozen artichoke
   bottoms (about 850 grams)

3 *Tablespoons chopped fresh*
   tarragon, or 2 to 3 teaspoons
   crushed dried tarragon
½ *cup chicken stock*
Chopped fresh tarragon or
   parsley for garnish

While chicken is in the oven for the initial baking, melt the butter in a saucepan over medium heat. When hot, add the mushrooms and sauté for 2 to 3 minutes. Reduce heat to low, and add the artichoke bottoms and tarragon. Cook gently in the butter until the artichokes are hot. Remove from the heat, cover, and set aside. When the initial baking is completed, remove the skillet from the oven. Add the white meat to the skillet, and using a slotted spoon, arrange the artichokes and mushrooms over the chicken. Cover, and return to the oven for the final baking of 12 to 15 minutes. When chicken is done (see page 94), arrange on a heated platter with the garnish.

Place the skillet with the juices from the chicken over medium-high heat. Add the stock, and reduce for a minute or two to about half its original volume, stirring the bits that are encrusted on the bottom of the pan into the sauce. Strain the sauce, and pour over the chicken and garnish. Sprinkle with additional chopped fresh tarragon or parsley. Serve immediately.

Accompany with buttered green beans, fresh peas, and boiled new potatoes.

The sweetness of the tarragon and artichoke bottoms calls for a fruity, slightly sweet white wine such as Liebfraumilch or a California Johannisberg Riesling.

Makes 4 to 6 servings.

CHICKEN MARENGO

❖❖❖

Very few dishes have legendary histories so well recorded that they can be assigned birthdays. Chicken Marengo is one of them. On June 4, 1800, the French forces under Napoleon defeated Austria at Marengo (a very small town seventy miles northwest of Genoa), and Austrian dominion over Italy was toppled. On the eve of that "great" battle, Napoleon's chef allegedly prepared dinner from what he could find in the Italian countryside: some tomatoes, garlic, and certainly olive oil, maybe some mushrooms, a few crayfish, a loaf of bread, some eggs, and a chicken. It was from these not-meager findings that Napoleon's chef created chicken Marengo, more famous today than the battle itself.

Olive oil
4 slices white bread (for croutons)
12 medium-sized shrimp
1 2½- to 3-pound chicken, cut into serving pieces (see page 224) (1¼–1½ kilograms)
¼ pound mushrooms, stems removed and cut in quarters (125 grams)
1 garlic clove, finely chopped
½ cup chicken stock
¼ cup white wine
2 tomatoes, peeled, seeded, and coarsely chopped
2 teaspoons tomato purée or tomato paste
Salt
Freshly ground black pepper
Oil for frying the eggs
4 eggs, preferably small or medium in size
Chopped parsley for garnish

First prepare the garnish.

Place a skillet or frying pan over medium-high heat and add enough olive oil to generously film the bottom of the pan. While the oil is heating, trim the crusts from the bread and cut diagonally in half to make 8 triangles. When the oil is hot, sauté the bread, 3 or 4 triangles at a time, until crisp and golden brown, turning once or twice during the minute and a half to two minutes of cooking. Drain on paper toweling. Sauté the remaining bread in the same way, adding more oil if necessary.

Add the shrimp to boiling salted water. When the water returns to a boil, boil the shrimp for 3 minutes. Drain, and immediately run under cold water until cool enough to handle easily. Remove the shells, and although not necessary, remove the black vein if you wish.

Sauté the chicken brown as directed in the master recipe (see page 93). When chicken has completed its final baking, remove from the oven and reset the oven to 150° F. to 200° F. Heat a large platter on the bottom shelf in the oven. Arrange the chicken on one side of a baking sheet lined with a brown paper bag, place the croutons and shrimp on the other side, cover loosely with a piece of aluminum foil, and place on the upper shelf of the oven to keep warm while the sauce and eggs are prepared.

Pour all the juices from the skillet and reserve. Add 2 or 3 tablespoons of olive oil, and sauté the mushrooms over medium-high heat for 2 to 3 minutes. Remove the mushrooms and reserve. Add the garlic and sauté for a minute or two over medium-low heat without browning. Now add the reserved juices, the stock, and white wine. Raise heat to medium-high and reduce by one third, scraping the brown-encrusted bits from the bottom of the pan into the sauce. Stir in the chopped tomatoes and tomato paste, and add the sautéed mushrooms. Season with salt and pepper to taste. Reduce heat to very low and simmer gently while the eggs are fried.

Pour an inch of oil into a saucepan and heat to 300° F. Break an egg into a small cup. Dip the cup into the hot oil, and at the same time gently pour out the egg. Using a large soupspoon, roll the egg against the side of the pan to give it a round shape. Cook for 1 minute.

Remove with a slotted spoon, trim any ragged edges, and drain on the paper-lined baking sheet. Fry the remaining 3 eggs in the same way. If you have never fried an egg this way, it's a good idea to practice with a few before embarking on this dish for the first time.

Now—for the final assembly and presentation. Arrange the chicken in the center of the platter: legs and thighs on the bottom, then the breasts, and finally the wings on top. Surround the chicken with the croutons. Place a fried egg on every second crouton, and 3 shrimp on each of the others. Spoon a little sauce over the shrimp, and pour the remaining sauce over the chicken. Sprinkle the eggs and chicken with chopped parsley. This is a dish that can proudly be presented at tableside!

Serve with tender young buttered green beans or peas. Oddly enough, a dish with such an astonishing pedigree does not deserve an equally pedigreed wine. There are simply too many varying flavors trying to marry in the mouth already without adding yet another combating flavor. I would probably serve either a robust Barolo from Italy's Piedmont or a Côtes du Rhône from France. Within the historic context of the Marengo battle, either of these would be nationally correct.

Makes 8 servings.

CHICKEN PANNÉ

———— ❖❖❖ ————

Chicken Panné, or panned chicken, is sautéed breaded chicken breasts, flamed in Cognac, and served with a bouquet of parsley and a wedge of lemon. Very much like wiener schnitzel, but better!

4 *to 6 chicken breasts, boned* *and skinned*	*2 eggs*
½ *cup flour*	*1 cup fresh bread crumbs*
2 *teaspoons salt*	*6 Tablespoons butter*
1 *teaspoon freshly ground* *black pepper*	*3 Tablespoons Cognac*
	Parsley sprigs for garnish
	Lemon wedges for garnish

Place the chicken breasts between sheets of waxed paper. With a heavy cleaver or meat pounder, flatten the breasts to a thickness of about ¼ inch. Trim any ragged edges with a sharp knife.

Mix the flour, salt, and pepper on a plate. Beat the eggs well in a bowl, and place next to the flour. Place the bread crumbs on a plate next to the eggs.

Carefully peel the waxed paper from each breast. One at a time, roll in flour, patting any excess, dip into the eggs, allowing any excess to drip back into the bowl, then coat in the bread crumbs, patting them firmly onto the chicken. Chill for at least 1 hour before sautéing.

Melt the butter in a large pan over medium heat. When hot, add the chicken and sauté until a golden brown, turning occasionally during the 3 to 4 minutes it will take to cook the chicken. If your pan is not large enough to hold all four breasts comfortably, sauté them in two batches.

When all the chicken has been sautéed, warm the Cognac in a separate pan. *Carefully* ignite, and pour over the chicken, gently shaking the pan back and forth until the flames die.

Arrange on a heated platter, garnish with parsley and lemon wedges, and serve immediately.

Serve with peas, zucchini steamed in butter, or a vegetable

stew like ratatouille. Well, it isn't often you'll come across Austrian wines in this country, but as long as your menu is featuring an Austrian dish such as a schnitzel, why not see if you can find a dry light Austrian wine such as Grüner Veltliner? An excellent alternative would be a Chénin Blanc from California.

Serves 4 to 6, if you're planning one breast for each person. If the breasts are large, split in half lengthwise, and serve half a breast per person.

CHICKEN CORDON BLEU

————— ❖❖❖ —————

A very popular dish in this country is veal cordon bleu. This variation, using chicken breasts instead of veal, is at least as good, and sometimes I think, better. But the real key to this dish is in using a good ham and a fine cheese—with bland, boiled ham slices and plastic-wrapped processed cheese, chicken cordon bleu is not much to get excited about.

8 *suprêmes (boneless and skinless half-breasts, see page 233)*
4 *thin slices of ham (a prosciutto, if available, is great, or a good country ham, perhaps one from Mississippi or Virginia)*
4 *thin slices of a good Swiss cheese, or perhaps a Gruyère*

2 *eggs, beaten*
½ *cup flour*
2 *teaspoons salt*
1 *teaspoon freshly ground black pepper*
½ *cup dried bread crumbs*
6 *Tablespoons butter*
1 *cup Basic Brown Sauce (see page 216)*

Place each suprême between sheets of waxed paper. With a heavy cleaver or meat pounder, flatten quite thin, at least to ¼ inch. Trim any ragged edges with a sharp knife.

Lay one of the pieces flat on the counter. Place a slice of ham and a slice of cheese on top of it, and trim the ham and cheese so that there is a border of chicken around them, about ¼ inch on all sides. Brush the border with beaten eggs. Cover with a second piece of chicken, pressing the edges together. Trim the edges so that the two pieces of chicken are the same size all round.

Repeat with the remaining breasts.

Mix the flour, salt, and pepper on a plate. Place the dish with the beaten eggs next to it, and the bread crumbs on a plate next to that. Carefully coat each breast in flour, gently patting off any excess, then dip in the beaten eggs, and roll in the bread crumbs, pressing the bread crumbs firmly onto the chicken. Repeat until all the chicken has been breaded.

Melt the butter in a large skillet over medium heat. When hot, add the chicken and sauté for a minute or so. Turn, and continue sautéing, turning occasionally, until the chicken is nicely colored to a golden brown, 6 to 8 minutes in all.

Remove to a heated platter and add the brown sauce to the skillet. Stir, scraping any brown-encrusted bits on the bottom of the skillet into the sauce. When the sauce is hot, pour over the chicken and serve immediately.

Serve with boiled potatoes, a green vegetable, and a light, somewhat fruity red wine such as Beaujolais from France or a Gamay Beaujolais from California.

Serves 4, but can easily be halved again to serve 6, or doubled to serve 8, depending upon appetites and what else is served.

CHICKEN AND OYSTER SAUTÉ FOUR SEASONS

—— ❖❖❖ ——

One of the most exciting dining rooms anywhere in the world is the pool room at the Four Seasons in New York City. This magnificent chicken sauté, cooked for two at tableside, was created by Oreste Carnevale, the maître d', and is served on a bed of homemade green noodles cooked *al dente*.

As one can see from the list of ingredients, this recipe requires a whole chicken, most of which is not used in the recipe. It also presupposes an open bottle of Cognac, a good bottle of Champagne on hand, and a resident *saucier* to prepare the two sauces —plus someone to spend the afternoon rolling out fresh green noodles!

It is a beautiful, sensual dish that requires care and patience in the assembly of the ingredients. I like to think of it as the perfect dish for lovers to share on a cold winter night—either at home or in the warmth of the Four Seasons.

8 Tablespoons butter
2 shallots, finely chopped
1 large canned cèpe, sliced
The 2 small fillets of a chicken breast located on the underside of the breast, and the 2 "oysters" located in the base of the back
4 ounces cooked crayfish tails (125 grams), shells removed and reserved for sauce Nantua

1 teaspoon green peppercorns, crushed with the flat side of a knife and finely chopped
3 Tablespoons Cognac
¼ cup Champagne
4 oysters, with their liquor
¼ cup Basic Brown Sauce (see page 216)
¼ cup sauce Nantua (see note)
Salt
Freshly ground black pepper

Place the butter in a large skillet over medium-high heat. When very hot, add the shallots, cèpes, chicken, crayfish tails, and green peppercorns. Sauté quickly, not more than a minute or two, tossing and turning all the ingredients in the pan so that they cook evenly. In a separate pan, warm the Cognac. Carefully ignite, and pour into the skillet. Shake the skillet back and forth until the flames die. Reduce heat to medium-low, and add the Champagne. Cook for another 15 seconds, then add the oysters and oyster liquor. Toss the oysters gently in the pan for about 10 seconds, then add the brown sauce and the sauce Nantua. Stir or shake until the sauces combine with the liquid in the pan. Taste, and season with salt and pepper. Pour onto a bed of green noodles, and serve immediately.

A crusty homemade bread with butter is all this dish needs as an accompaniment. Follow Four Seasons' co-owner Paul Kovi's advice and serve a *brut* Champagne from France.

NOTE: To prepare a sauce Nantua, make a white sauce with half heavy cream and half fish stock. Enrich the sauce with 6 tablespoons of shellfish butter, made by pounding, with mortar and pestle, the reserved crayfish shells with 6 tablespoons of butter, ¼ teaspoon of salt, and a little freshly ground black pepper. Press the butter through a sieve to remove the shells. Chill butter.

ALEX KOMEN'S CHICKEN WITH SESAME SEEDS

—————— ❖❖❖ ——————

Alex is a friend from Amsterdam and a frequent guest in my home. In an attempt to create something vaguely Dutch for dinner one night, I came up with this simple and delicious recipe. The toasted sesame seeds, with their warm, golden-honey color and lovely fragrance, are a nice complement in taste and texture to a delicately flavored chicken breast.

2 ounces sesame seeds, about ¼ cup (50 grams)	*Flour*
	6 Tablespoons oil
4 suprêmes (boneless and skinless half-breasts) (see page 233)	*Salt*
	Freshly ground black pepper

Place the sesame seeds in a large skillet over medium heat. Shake the pan gently back and forth for 3 or 4 minutes until the seeds have toasted to a light, golden brown. Immediately pour onto a cold plate.

Place each suprême between two sheets of waxed paper or plastic wrap. With a heavy cleaver or meat pounder, flatten the chicken to an even thickness of about ¼ inch. Remove the paper and trim any ragged edges with a sharp knife. Dust the chicken lightly in flour, shaking off any excess.

Pour the oil into the skillet and set it over medium-low heat. When hot, add the chicken and sauté for 3 to 4 minutes, turning once or twice, until the chicken is cooked through and only lightly colored. Remove from the skillet, sprinkle lightly with salt and pepper, and roll in the toasted sesame seeds. Serve immediately.

Serve with garlic-flavored potatoes, a mixed green salad, and a full-bodied and fruity but dry white wine such as a Meursault or a Puligny-Montrachet from France's Burgundy region.

Serves 4, but can easily be halved again to serve 6, or doubled to serve 8.

SOUTHERN FRIED CHICKEN

MASTER RECIPE

For some, rhubarb heralded the arrival of spring. For others it was the first signs of pinkness in the berries on the local knoll. But to a Southerner it was that Sunday morning when he returned home from the fields for breakfast and the door opened to a house filled with the fragrance of tender, young spring chickens being fried. Today we don't have to wait for spring to enjoy a luscious, tender chicken fried to perfection—or for that matter, to eat rhubarb or fresh berries.

1 *cup flour*
2 *teaspoons salt*
1 *teaspoon freshly ground black pepper*
1 *2½- to 3-pound chicken, cut into serving pieces (see page 224)* (1¼–1½ kilograms)
Lard for frying, about 2 pounds (1 kilogram)

CREAM GRAVY

3 *Tablespoons flour*
2 *cups light cream*
Salt
Freshly ground black pepper
Parsley or watercress for garnish

Preheat the oven to its lowest setting, 150° F.–200° F. Line a baking sheet or ovenproof dish with absorbent paper, either paper toweling or a brown paper bag, and place on a shelf in the middle of the oven. A serving platter can be heated on the bottom shelf.

Mix the flour, salt, and pepper in a large bowl. Roll the chicken, one piece at a time, in the seasoned flour, patting the flour firmly and generously onto the chicken.

Heat the lard to 350° F., either in a deep saucepan fitted with a frying basket or in a heavy, straight-sided skillet or electric frying pan with a wire rack on the bottom. There should be enough melted fat to reach at least an inch and a half above the rack or basket. It is important that there be a generous amount of fat for frying to ensure that the chicken seals properly and cooks quickly and evenly.

Carefully place the dark meat in the preheated fat, making sure that no two pieces are touching. Fry for 3 to 4 minutes, then turn with a pair of tongs and continue frying, turning occasionally so that the chicken browns nicely on all sides, about 10 to 12 minutes in all.

TEST FOR DONENESS: Remove one of the pieces of chicken and insert an instantly registering thermometer into the thickest part of the meat without touching the bone. It should register 165° F. When done, transfer the chicken to the paper-lined baking sheet in the oven to drain and keep warm while the remaining chicken is fried.

Check the temperature of the fat; it should still be 350° F.

Add the white meat, again being certain that none of the pieces are touching. Fry for 2 to 3 minutes, then turn and continue frying, turning once or twice more, until the chicken is nicely browned on all sides, about 7 to 8 minutes in all. Remove a piece of the breast, and test for doneness as for the dark meat, but this time the thermometer should register 140° F. When done, add to the chicken in the oven to drain, and keep warm while the gravy is prepared.

Pour off all but 3 or 4 tablespoons of the lard, leaving as many of the flavorful, brown crusty bits as possible in the bottom of the skillet. Place over medium-low heat or reset thermostat to medium-low, and stir in the flour. Simmer for 3 to 4 minutes to remove the starchy taste of the raw flour, then stir in the cream. Increase the heat to medium, and continue stirring until the gravy comes to a boil and thickens. Season with salt and pepper to taste, reduce heat, and simmer for 5 minutes. Pour into a sauceboat, and pass with the chicken arranged on a heated platter with a large bouquet of fresh parsley or watercress at each end.

Serve with rice, green onions poached in butter or a boiled green vegetable, and baking-powder biscuits or cornbread sticks. Southern Fried Chicken can be served with either a light red wine, perhaps a Beaujolais Nouveau, which is available from November to May when it still has the freshness and zest of its youth, or with a dry white wine such as a Chardonnay from France or California.

Makes 6 to 8 servings.

If you are frying a lot of chicken—say, 2 or 3 times the amount suggested in the recipe—it might be a good idea to use two frying pans at once.

One of my favorite variations on this recipe, though it does require that you have a frying pan large enough to hold all the chicken, is to add about ¼ pound of unsalted butter to the lard for the last 5 minutes of frying. The crust of the chicken will absorb the butter, and though it won't be as crisp as it would without the butter, it certainly will be richer and more luscious. The one drawback to adding the butter is that the lard will burn easily if reused—a sacrifice I usually feel worth making.

MISSISSIPPI FRIED CHICKEN

—— ❖❖❖ ——

Although it would cause many a staunch Southerner to screech with fear, this fried chicken is made with baking powder mixed into the flour. It's an interesting variation that produces a lighter, more delicate crust and is delicious with the rich onion gravy.

1 *cup flour*
2 *teaspoons salt*
1 *teaspoon freshly ground
  black pepper*
½ *teaspoon baking powder*
1 *2½- to 3-pound chicken, cut*

*in serving pieces (see page
224) (1¼–1½ kilograms)*
1 *cup heavy cream*
Oil for frying, approximately
  1½ quarts (1½ liters)

ONION GRAVY

1 *large onion, chopped*
Pinch of dried thyme
3 *Tablespoons flour*
2 *cups chicken stock*

Salt
Freshly ground black pepper
Freshly grated nutmeg
(optional)

Preheat oven to 150° F.–200° F. Line a baking sheet with absorbent paper, and place on a shelf in the middle of the oven. A serving platter can be heated on the bottom shelf.

Combine the flour, salt, pepper, and baking powder in a plastic or paper bag and mix well. Dip the chicken in the cream, drain, then shake in the bag until evenly coated in flour. Gently shake off any excess flour.

Heat enough oil to 350° F. to fill a frying pan to a depth of about 2 inches above the rack. Carefully place the dark meat in the hot oil. Fry for 3 to 4 minutes, then turn with tongs and continue frying, turning occasionally until chicken is nicely browned, about 10 to 12 minutes in all. Test for doneness (see page 112).

Place the cooked chicken on the paper-lined baking sheet and return to the oven to drain and keep warm while the remaining chicken is fried.

Add the white meat to the skillet. Fry for 2 to 3 minutes, then turn and continue frying, turning once or twice more, until chicken is nicely browned, about 7 or 8 minutes in all. Test for doneness (see page 112). When done, add to the chicken in the oven to drain and keep warm while the gravy is prepared.

Pour out all but about 4 tablespoons of oil from the frying pan, leaving as many of the browned bits of breading in the oil as possible. Place over medium heat or reset thermostat to 325° F. Add the onion and sauté until tender and translucent, about 5 minutes. Add a pinch of thyme and sprinkle with the flour. Reduce heat to medium-low and simmer for 3 to 4 minutes, stirring the whole time. Stir in the chicken stock, raise the heat, and bring the gravy to a boil, still stirring. When the gravy has reached a full boil and thickened, reduce the heat and simmer for 5 minutes. Season with salt and pepper to taste, and a little nutmeg if you wish.

Pour the gravy into a large sauceboat and pass with the chicken. I think the onion gravy is good on the chicken, but even more exciting when poured over steaming rice. Serve with a colorful mixed salad. A somewhat full-bodied, slightly fruity red Beaujolais or red wine of Burgundy would be lovely with this dish, as would a California Zinfandel.

Makes 6 to 8 servings.

UNORTHODOX SOUTHERN FRIED CHICKEN

❖❖❖

My housekeeper, Betty Wood, is warm and patient with me as I strew pots, pans, and everything else about the kitchen in the course of a day's work. After several days of quietly watching me fry chicken, she said, "Don't you ever use matzo meal when you fry chicken?" And now I do.

2 eggs
½ cup milk
½ cup flour
1½ teaspoons salt
½ teaspoon freshly ground
black pepper
1 cup matzo meal

1 2½- to 3-pound frying
chicken, cut into serving
pieces (see page 224) (1¼–
1½ kilograms)
Oil for frying, approximately
1½ quarts (1½ liters)

Preheat oven to 150° F.–200° F. Line a baking sheet with absorbent paper and place on a shelf in the middle of the oven. A serving platter can be heated on the bottom shelf.

Beat the eggs and milk in a large bowl until well combined.

Mix the flour, salt, and pepper in a second bowl. Pour the matzo meal onto a plate. First, roll the chicken, one piece at a time, in the seasoned flour and shake off any excess, then dip in the milk and eggs, and finally, roll in the matzo meal. Press the matzo meal firmly onto the chicken.

Heat enough oil to 350° F. to fill a frying pan to a depth of about 2 inches above the rack. Carefully add the dark meat to the hot fat. Fry for 3 or 4 minutes, then turn with tongs and continue frying, turning occasionally until the chicken is nicely browned, about 10 to 12 minutes in all. Test for doneness (see page 112).

Place the cooked chicken on the paper-lined baking sheet; return to the oven to drain and keep warm while the remaining white meat is cooked.

Add the white meat to the hot fat and fry for 3 to 4 minutes. Turn and continue frying, turning once or twice more, until chicken is nicely browned, about 7 or 8 minutes in all. Test for doneness (see page 112). Drain on the baking sheet, then arrange on a heated platter.

Serve with mashed potatoes, beaten biscuits, and perhaps some eggplant or zucchini, and a medium to full-bodied red wine from Italy's Piedmont region such as Bersano Barbaresco.

Makes 6 to 8 servings.

In Virginia, crushed cracker crumbs would be used in place of matzo meal, and a cream gravy would be served with the chicken.

CHICKEN TABASCO

——— ❖❖❖ ———

This is one of my favorite kinds of fried chicken. It can be made with a cream gravy and served hot, but I like it better cold, that is, at room temperature, and it is my favorite picnic chicken. The Tabasco spices it up a little, but does not really make it hot. And you may be surprised to learn that using 4 ounces of Tabasco will not make it four times as hot as if you'd only used 1 ounce.

4 *ounces Tabasco sauce*
(about 125 milliliters)
1 *quart milk* (1 liter)
1 2½- *to 3-pound chicken, cut
into serving pieces (see page
224)* (1¼–1½ kilograms)
1 *cup whole-wheat flour*

⅓ *cup white flour*
2 *teaspoons salt*
1 *teaspoon freshly ground
black pepper*
Lard for frying, about 2
pounds (1 kilogram)

Combine the Tabasco and milk in a large bowl, and add the chicken. Marinate for 3 to 4 hours before frying.

If serving hot, preheat the oven to 150° F.–200° F. Line a baking sheet with absorbent paper and place on a shelf in the middle of the oven to keep the chicken warm while the remaining pieces are fried. A serving platter can be placed on the bottom shelf. If chicken is to be served cold or taken on a picnic, simply drain it on absorbent paper in a cool part of the kitchen.

Mix the flours, salt, and pepper in a plastic or paper bag and add the chicken, 2 or 3 pieces at a time. Shake until the chicken is well coated in flour, gently tapping off the excess flour as the chicken is removed from the bag.

Heat enough lard to 350° F. to fill a frying pan to a depth of about 2 inches above the rack. Carefully add the dark meat to the hot fat. Fry for 3 to 4 minutes, then turn with tongs and continue frying, turning occasionally until chicken is nicely browned, about 10 to 12 minutes. Test for doneness (see page 112).

Add the white meat to the skillet. Fry for 2 to 3 minutes, then turn and continue frying, turning only once or twice more, until chicken is nicely browned, about 7 or 8 minutes in all. Test for doneness (see page 112).

You will probably want to accompany this somewhat hot dish with a cold wine, so your best bet would be to stick to a sturdy white wine, served well chilled. A Sicilian white Corvo would be very nice, as would a Verdicchio, also from Italy. Excellent with this chicken is a bitter leaf vegetable like chard or collards, and some steaming rice cooked in chicken stock. A cream gravy would go nicely, and if you're daring, try adding half a cup of the marinade to it. For picnics, serve with leeks, asparagus, or broccoli vinaigrette, and perhaps some homemade yeast biscuits. Cold beer can be just as good for picnics as wine.

Makes 6 to 8 servings.

CHICKEN KIEV

————— ❖❖❖ —————

Chicken Kiev has become so popular that it is sometimes found in supermarket freezers and is available from certain mail-order houses. Named for the Ukrainian city of Kiev, it is a boned chicken breast, flattened slightly and then stuffed with butter, breaded, and fried. It is one of the few dishes that actually has its moment of drama right at the table. As your knife first cuts into it, the butter spurts out onto the plate! Chicken Kiev is usually filled with an herbed butter. Use a plain butter, the mixed herb butter suggested below, or any of the flavored butters on pages 10–16.

1 *recipe mixed herb butter*   ½ *teaspoon freshly ground*
   (see page 12)   *black pepper*
4 *whole chicken breasts,*   2 *eggs*
   boned and skinned   1 *cup dried bread crumbs*
½ *cup flour*   *Oil for frying*
1 *teaspoon salt*

Shape the butter into 3-inch cylinders and place in the freezer.

Place each breast between two sheets of waxed paper. With a heavy cleaver or meat pounder, flatten the breasts to a thickness of about ¼ inch. Trim any ragged edges with a sharp knife.

Mix the flour, salt, and pepper on a plate. Beat the eggs together in a large bowl, set next to the flour, and place the bread crumbs on a plate next to that.

Heat enough oil to 350° F. to fill a frying pan to a depth of about 2 inches above the rack.

Carefully peel the waxed paper from the chicken. Place a butter cylinder on the flattened breast, about a third of the way in from the side. Roll the smaller side of the chicken over the butter. Next, fold the right and left sides over it. Now fold the remaining edge around the "package," being certain that the butter is well sealed inside the breast.

Carefully roll the chicken in the seasoned flour, gently patting off any excess. Dip into the eggs, allowing any excess egg to drip off. Finally, roll in the bread crumbs, patting the crumbs firmly onto the chicken. Refrigerate while breading the remaining breasts. All of this can be done several hours or a day ahead, if you wish.

Place the chicken in the hot oil. Fry, turning occasionally and carefully, until the chicken is nicely browned, about 6 to 8 minutes. Remove from the oil and drain on paper toweling. Serve immediately on a bed of rice.

This exciting dish can be served with either a white wine or a red, but in any case the wine should be elegant and distinguished, such as one of the great white Montrachets from Burgundy or, in the red family, a fine château-bottled Bordeaux from the Médoc region.

Makes 4 servings, but can be halved again to serve 6, or doubled to serve 8.

CHINESE CHICKEN WINGS

Chinese chicken wings are the greatest little hors d'oeuvre I have ever served. They are great "finger food." Three of the four bones are removed, all of the meat is shaped in a ball at the end of the one remaining bone, and then they are breaded and fried. Kids love them because they look like lollypops.

1 *cup flour*	½ *cup milk*
1 *Tablespoon salt*	1 *cup dried bread crumbs*
1 *teaspoon freshly ground*	*Oil for frying*
black pepper	24 *boned wings (see directions*
2 *eggs*	*on page 236)*

Mix the flour, salt, and pepper on a plate. Beat the eggs and milk together in a small bowl, and spread the bread crumbs on a plate next to it.

Roll the ball of meat, not the bone, in the seasoned flour, gently patting off any excess; then dip into the egg-and-milk mixture, and allow the excess liquid to drain back into the bowl. Now roll in the bread crumbs, patting the crumbs firmly onto the meat. Set aside until all the wings have been breaded.

Heat enough oil to 350° F. to fill a frying pan to a depth of 2 inches above the rack. Add the breaded wings, 6 or 8 at a time, depending on the size of the skillet. Do not crowd them. Turn the wings with tongs 3 or 4 times during the frying so that they brown evenly. The total cooking time should only be 6 to 8 minutes. When done, remove to a paper-lined baking sheet to drain, and repeat with the next batch.

Test for doneness by inserting an instantly registering thermometer into the center of the meat. When it registers 140° F., the chicken wings are done.

When these are served as an hors d'oeuvre, a dry white, flinty wine such as French Chablis would be fine, as would a California Chardonnay.

Makes 24 wings.

5

CASSEROLES AND BAKED DISHES

———————— ❖❖❖ ————————

THE RECIPES in this chapter are all cooked in an oven. I have a personal fondness for these recipes because once the oven door closes, I am free to set the table, prepare the vegetables, or visit with my guests.

MARION CUNNINGHAM'S
CHICKEN WITH
BACKYARD VEGETABLES

———————— ❖❖❖ ————————

Marion, who has recently spent four years revising *The Fanny Farmer Cookbook*, teaches cooking classes from her home in Walnut Creek, California. This is one of her recipes, which I have borrowed—with her permission. It is a favorite of mine and will soon become a favorite of yours, even if you don't have Marion's backyard.

10 *Tablespoons butter*
½ *teaspoon crushed dried thyme*
1 *to 2 garlic cloves, finely chopped*
1 *3- to 3½-pound chicken* (about 1½ kilograms)
Salt
Freshly ground black pepper
16 *2-inch pieces of potato*

16 *small white onions, carefully peeled without removing too much of the root end*
6 *medium-sized carrots, cut into 2-inch lengths*
4 *medium-sized zucchini or yellow squash, cut into 2-inch pieces*

Preheat oven to 375° F.

Beat 6 tablespoons of the butter with the thyme and garlic until light and pale green in color.

Carefully lift the skin from the breast, and using your fingers, pierce the thin membrane that holds the skin to the meat. Slide your fingers under the skin, gradually working them around until the skin has been lifted from the breast, thighs and legs. Rub about half of the thyme-flavored butter under the skin. Smooth the skin back into place, and truss (see page 221). Smear the remaining thyme-flavored butter over the outside of the chicken. Sprinkle with salt and pepper, massaging the salt and pepper into the buttery skin.

Melt the remaining butter in a large skillet over medium heat. When hot, add the chicken and brown on all sides. Transfer the chicken to a deep casserole, and set aside.

Add the potatoes to the same skillet in which the chicken was browned, and sauté until lightly browned. With a slotted spoon, transfer the potatoes to the casserole with the chicken. Brown the onions and carrots in the same way, adding a little more butter to the skillet as needed, and transfer them to the casserole. Brown the squash and set aside. Cover the casserole with a tight-fitting lid and bake for 25 minutes. Add the squash, and bake 20 minutes longer.

Test for doneness: Insert an instantly registering thermometer into the thickest part of the thigh without touching the bone. It should register 165° F. If not, return to the oven for 5 to 10 minutes, and test again.

Serve the chicken with its accompanying vegetables. This dish is robust enough to be married with a full-bodied, round red wine with a big bouquet and appealing style, such as one from Pomerol or Margaux.

Makes 6 to 8 servings.

CHICKEN PARMESAN

This recipe is named for one of the three essential cheeses in Italian cooking (the other two being mozzarella and ricotta).

It is a delicious dish when made with freshly grated Parmesan. The best Parmesan is imported from Italy and purchased in chunks that you grate as you need.

3 *Tablespoons oil*
1 *2½- to 3½-pound chicken, cut into serving pieces (see page 224) (1¼–1½ kilograms)*
1 *teaspoon salt*
½ *teaspoon freshly ground black pepper*
1½ *cups chicken stock*
1½ *cups dry white wine*

2 *garlic cloves, bruised by hitting them with the flat side of a cook's knife*
1 *bay leaf, crumbled*
3 *Tablespoons butter*
3 *Tablespoons flour*
Salt
Freshly ground black pepper
1 *cup freshly grated Parmesan cheese (50 grams)*

Preheat oven to 350° F.

Pour the oil into a skillet over medium-high heat. Pat the chicken dry. When the oil is hot, add 3 or 4 pieces of the chicken, skin side down. Sear the chicken quickly, turning once or twice so that it browns evenly. Sear the remaining chicken in the same way, adding more oil if necessary. It is better to do this in several batches than to crowd the pan.

Season the chicken on all sides with salt and pepper. Arrange in a casserole or baking dish, skin side up, and add the stock, wine, garlic, and bay leaf. Cover, and bake in a 350° F. oven for 35 minutes.

While the chicken is baking, melt the butter in a saucepan over medium-low heat. Stir in the flour and simmer for 3 to 4 minutes to remove the starchy taste of the raw flour. When chicken is cooked, remove from the oven and reset to 450° F.–500° F. Arrange the chicken on a plate and strain the cooking liquid into the saucepan. Increase the heat, and continue stirring until the sauce comes to a boil and thickens. Season with salt and pepper to taste. Reduce heat to very low and simmer while the chicken is coated in cheese.

Spread the Parmesan onto a plate. Roll the chicken in the grated cheese, pressing it firmly onto the chicken. Arrange the chicken, skin side up, in the baking dish and return to the oven, uncovered, until the cheese melts, about 3 to 4 minutes.

When the cheese is completely melted, arrange the chicken on a heated platter and serve immediately. The sauce in the baking dish can be spooned over the chicken or passed separately. Serve with rice or potatoes and a green vegetable.

This dish may not be Italian, but without Italian Parmiggiano it couldn't exist, so I recommend a fine Italian wine, a Riserva Chianti *classico*.

Makes 6 to 8 servings.

CHICKEN WITH HAZELNUTS AND BUTTERMILK GRAVY

———— ❖❖❖ ————

There is a tendency to toss almonds on everything in sight while the humble hazelnut lies ignored and forgotten. The beautiful, rich fragrance of hazelnuts, which marry so well with the buttermilk gravy, makes this one of my favorite recipes.

The variation which follows this recipe calls for pecans and a cream gravy. It is a good dish. But it is nowhere near as exciting as the one made with hazelnuts!

12 *Tablespoons butter*
12 *ounces toasted hazelnuts, very finely chopped* (350 grams)
1 *Tablespoon salt*
2 *teaspoons freshly ground black pepper*

2 *cups buttermilk*
2 2½- *to 3-pound chickens, cut into serving pieces (see page 224)* (1¼–1½ *kilograms*)

THE GRAVY

3 *Tablespoons flour*
1 *cup milk*

Salt
Freshly ground black pepper

Put the butter in an ovenproof dish or casserole and place in a cold oven. Set the oven to 350° F. The butter will melt as the oven is preheating.

Combine the hazelnuts, salt, and pepper on a plate and mix well. Place the buttermilk in a bowl next to it.

Dip the chicken into the buttermilk, using your hand to scrape any excess back into the bowl. Roll in the seasoned hazelnuts, pressing the nuts firmly onto the chicken. Reserve 1 cup buttermilk for the gravy. Remove the baking dish from the oven and place the chicken in it, turning each piece in the melted butter to coat it on all sides, and finally arranging the chicken skin side up.

Bake for 1¼ hours in a fully preheated 350° F. oven. Baste every 15 or 20 minutes with butter from the casserole. When done, arrange the chicken on a heated platter and prepare the gravy.

Pour 3 to 4 tablespoons of butter from the casserole into a saucepan. Spoon as many of the nuts as possible into the butter. Place over medium-low heat, and stir in the flour. Simmer for 3 to 4 minutes to remove the starchy taste of the raw flour. Stir in the milk and reserved buttermilk. Increase the heat, and continue stirring until the sauce comes to a boil and thickens. Season with salt and pepper to taste. Simmer for 1 minute, then pour over the chicken and serve immediately.

With the fragrant taste of the toasted hazelnuts and the slight tartness of the buttermilk gravy, I prefer simple vegetables like buttered broccoli and boiled potatoes, or perhaps rice. This dish is unusual enough to be served with a distinguished dry but fullish-bodied white Burgundy such as a Puligny-Montrachet.

Makes 6 to 8 servings.

CHICKEN WITH PECANS AND CREAM GRAVY: Substitute pecans for the hazelnuts, and use 1 cup of milk and 1 cup of heavy cream for the gravy.

CHICKEN BAKED IN CLAY

———— ❖❖❖ ————

Clay pots are used for cooking everything from wild game and poultry to roasts of beef, lamb, and pork. Even breads are sometimes baked in them. The clay pot, or "brick," that I use is just large enough to hold a 3-pound chicken. If you have never cooked in a clay pot before, there are two important things to remember: Never place the pot in a hot oven, and do not clean it with detergent, as the detergent taste will linger in the clay.

Cooking a whole chicken in a clay pot is really just another way of roasting it. But the clay brings the heat source so close to the chicken that it needs no basting or turning to produce a beautifully browned, crisp skin and juicy, tender meat.

1 *3-pound chicken* (1½ kilo-   *A small handful of parsley*
   grams)   *Half a lemon*
Salt   *Oil*
Freshly ground black pepper

Season the chicken inside and out with salt and pepper. Stuff the cavity with parsley and lemon. Truss the chicken (see page 221). Rub the outside of the chicken generously with oil. Place in the clay pot, which for the best results the chicken should completely fill; cover with the clay top.

Place in a *cold* oven. Set the oven to 500° F., and bake for 1½ hours. Test for doneness (see page 124). When done, place the chicken on a heated platter and remove the trussing string. Allow the chicken to rest at room temperature for 5 to 10 minutes so that the juices can retreat into the flesh. Pour the juices that have accumulated in the bottom of the clay pot into a sauceboat and pass separately. If the chicken is to be carved in the kitchen, spoon a tablespoon or two of the juices over each portion. Serve at once.

Accompany with any of the vegetables or wines suggested in the master recipe for roast chicken (see page 8).

Makes 4 to 6 servings.

This is another recipe where hundreds of small variations are possible. Butter can be used in place of the oil, any fresh herb can be used in place of the parsley. Or a piece of onion or a few garlic cloves can be added to the cavity. Use your imagination and what is on hand!

DEVILED THIGHS

———————— ❖❖❖ ————————

"Deviling" was popular in Britain during the eighteenth and nineteenth centuries, and is to a somewhat lesser degree in this century. The three traditional forms of deviling all shared two things in common: the meat was always cooked (or leftovers were used) before it was deviled, and the deviling sauce, whether white or brown, was always hot and spicy. It has now become increasingly popular in this country to devil fish as well as poultry, and deviled bones have begun to appear on restaurant menus.

4 *ounces Dijon mustard* (about 100 grams)	1 *cup dried bread crumbs*
¼ *cup oil*	8–12 *chicken thighs, or legs and thighs (plan two pieces per serving)*
2 *Tablespoons brown sugar*	
2 *garlic cloves, finely chopped*	
½ *teaspoon freshly ground black pepper*	

Preheat oven to 375° F.

Combine the mustard, oil, brown sugar, garlic and pepper, and mix well. If you are using a fairly "tame" mustard, you should add a little salt and some cayenne or Tabasco to spice it up.

Brush the chicken with the deviling sauce, coating it on all sides. Roll in bread crumbs. Arrange in a lightly greased baking dish and bake in a 375° F. oven for 45 to 50 minutes.

Serve hot with potatoes and a mustard-flavored hollandaise sauce. As to the wine suggestion, so much depends of course on the time of day, and where and to whom you serve this dish. Picnics come to mind first, in which case I would serve a well-chilled, flavorful white wine, such as a Liebfraumilch or a Moselle from Germany. If you prefer a red wine, however, it should be a light, fruity one such as Beaujolais, though I would chill it for a few minutes before serving.

Makes 4 to 6 servings.

BAKED CHICKEN LEGS

❖❖❖

This recipe is simple, quick, and delicious. It can be made from any part of the chicken, though I prefer dark meat. If you choose to substitute white meat, reduce the baking time to about 30 minutes.

8 *Tablespoons butter*
4 *garlic cloves, finely chopped*
1 *teaspoon salt, if using*
  unsalted *butter*
½ *teaspoon freshly ground*
  black pepper

8–12 *drumsticks (plan two*
  pieces per serving)
Soy sauce
Freshly ground black pepper

Preheat oven to 375° F.

In a small saucepan, melt the butter over very low heat. Add the garlic, salt (if using unsalted butter), and pepper. Cook slowly for 3 or 4 minutes while preparing the drumsticks. If garlic should accidentally brown, do not worry. It will just add a slightly nutty taste to the butter, and the chicken will still be delicious.

Rub the drumsticks generously with soy sauce. Season with pepper.

Coat the bottom of a baking dish with 2 tablespoons of the garlic butter. Arrange the drumsticks in the baking dish, turning each in the garlic butter as it is added. Bake for 45 to 50 minutes, basting lavishly with the remaining butter every 10 to 15 minutes.

Serve with rice or mashed potatoes, and some zucchini or eggplant, and a hearty red wine, robust enough to stand up to these heady flavors—either a Côtes du Rhône from France, or a Barolo or Chianti *classico* from Italy.

Makes 4 to 6 servings.

BAKED CHICKEN

———— ❖❖❖ ————

There is a very dubious line that divides "roast" chicken from "baked" chicken. Originally, roasting meant the spitting of meat, fish, or vegetables that were to be cooked either directly over hot coals or immediately in front of a fire mounted on a reflecting screen. Baking was a term that implied sweets or pastries, cooked by indirect heat in a hollowed-out space in the fireplace, heated by wood and brushed clean before baking. But with the introduction of the modern oven in this century, the division between baking and roasting became blurred. I have made the division, albeit somewhat arbitrarily, in this way: when a chicken is whole, even if split down the back, and cooked by indirect heat in the oven, it is roasted. Baked chicken is cooked in exactly the same way, but the chicken has been cut into pieces.

2 2½- to 3-pound chickens,   *½ teaspoon freshly ground*
   split in half (see page 226)   *black pepper*
   (1¼–1½ kilograms)   *6 Tablespoons butter or oil*
1½ teaspoons salt

Preheat oven to 450° F.

Season the chicken with salt and pepper, and rub generously with 4 tablespoons butter or oil. Melt remaining butter for basting.

Place the chicken, skin side up, on a rack over a shallow roasting pan. Bake for 40 to 45 minutes, basting at least twice with the melted butter. Test for doneness by inserting an instantly registering thermometer into the thickest part of the thigh without touching the bone. It should register 165° F.

Accompany with any of the vegetables or wines suggested for roast chicken on page 8.

Makes 8 generous servings.

Any of the flavored butters or oils suggested for roast chicken on pages 10 to 18 can be used with baked chicken.

MARINATED BAKED CHICKEN

—————— ❖❖❖ ——————

The marinade in this dish is really just an uncooked barbecue sauce. And though my "sensitive and sophisticated" palate says the taste is a little overwhelming for the chicken, the hearty beast in me loves it!

¾ cup ketchup
¼ cup soy sauce
1 Tablespoon Worcestershire
   sauce
Juice of 1 small lemon
2 Tablespoons brown sugar

½ teaspoon salt
¼ teaspoon freshly ground
   black pepper
1 2½- to 3-pound chicken, cut
   into serving pieces (see page
   224) (1¼–1½ kilograms)

Combine the ketchup, soy sauce, Worcestershire, lemon juice, brown sugar, salt, and pepper in a large bowl, and mix well. Add the chicken, cover, and marinate overnight in the refrigerator, turning once or twice.

Preheat oven to 300° F.

Place the chicken and marinade in an ovenproof baking dish or casserole. Cover, and bake for 50 to 55 minutes.

Arrange the chicken on a heated platter, and bathe in the cooking juices. Serve with French fried potatoes or rice, and cold beer.

Makes 4 to 6 servings.

JUGGED CHICKEN

—————— ❖❖❖ ——————

"Jugging" was a way of preserving surplus game and a more than welcome alternative to "hanging" them. As the name suggests, the game were packed into jugs and a marinade was poured over them. The jugs were then stored in the cold cellar for leaner months. When I first tested this recipe, the purist in me made me try to pack the chicken into a glass jar. It didn't work, and I finally convinced the more reasonable side of myself that there was nothing wrong with marinating the chicken in a bowl covered with plastic wrap!

2 *cups water*
1 *cup dry white wine*
Juice of 1 *lemon*
2 *garlic cloves*
1 *Tablespoon chopped fresh*
  rosemary, or 1 *teaspoon*
  crushed dried rosemary
2 *teaspoons salt*
1 *teaspoon freshly ground*
  black pepper

1 *large onion, sliced*
1 2½- *to* 3-*pound chicken, cut*
  into serving pieces (see page
  224) (1¼–1½ *kilograms)*
3 *Tablespoons oil*
½ *teaspoon salt*
¼ *teaspoon freshly ground*
  black pepper

Combine the water, wine, lemon juice, garlic, rosemary, salt, and pepper in a large bowl. Mix well, and add the onion and chicken. Cover, and marinate in the refrigerator for 2–3 days, turning once or twice a day.

Remove the chicken and dry very well. Strain the marinade, and reserve 1 cup.

Pour the oil into a large skillet over medium heat. When very hot, add the chicken, 3 or 4 pieces at a time, skin side down. Brown the chicken, turning once or twice to ensure even coloring. Sprinkle with salt and pepper, and place in a casserole or baking dish.

Preheat oven to 325°.

When all the chicken has been browned, pour the reserved marinade into the skillet. Deglaze by scraping the brown-encrusted bits from the bottom of the skillet into the marinade. Pour over the chicken. Cover, and bake for 40 to 45 minutes.

To serve, arrange the chicken on a heated platter, spoon some of the juices from the casserole over the chicken, and sprinkle with chopped parsley. Accompany with boiled potatoes or buttered noodles, a crusty homemade bread, and a romaine salad.

Many people will tell you that this dish goes best with a crisp white wine. I don't agree, as I feel that the marinade imbues the chicken with too strong a flavor. I would choose a wine from Spain's northernmost region, Rioja, such as a Vina Pomal or

Clarete. However, if you prefer a white wine, make it a very full-flavored one such as a Gewürztraminer from Alsace in France.

Makes 4 to 6 servings.

This marinade is also excellent for grilled, broiled, or baked chicken.

OVEN-FRIED CHICKEN

———— ❖❖❖ ————

This is my version of a Fanny Farmer recipe for oven-baked chicken.

1 *cup flour*
1 *Tablespoon salt*
2 *teaspoons freshly ground*
   black pepper
1 2½- *to 3-pound chicken, cut*
   into serving pieces (or
   about 3 pounds chicken in
   pieces) (1¼–1½ *kilo-*
   grams)

6 *Tablespoons butter*
¼ *cup chicken stock*
4 *Tablespoons flour*
1 *cup chicken stock mixed*
   with 1 cup heavy cream
Salt
Freshly ground black pepper

Preheat oven to 450° F.

Combine the flour, salt, and pepper on a plate, and mix well. Roll the chicken in the seasoned flour, patting off any excess.

Melt the butter in a saucepan over medium-low heat and coat the bottom of a baking dish with 4 tablespoons of it. Add the chicken, turning each piece in the butter, and arrange them skin side up. Stir the ¼ cup of stock into the remaining butter, and reserve for basting. Bake the chicken for 30 to 35 minutes, basting generously and frequently with the butter and stock mixture. As white meat takes less time to cook, remove the breasts and wings after 20 to 25 minutes in the oven, and keep warm until the dark meat is ready.

When dark meat is done, remove from the oven and pour all the juices from the baking dish into the saucepan with any remaining basting butter. Place all of the chicken back in the baking dish, and return to the oven, now turned off. Leave the door slightly ajar. This will keep the chicken hot while the gravy is prepared.

Place the saucepan with the butter over medium-low heat.

With a wire whisk, stir the flour into the buttery brown juices, beating to prevent lumping. Simmer, stirring constantly, for 3 to 4 minutes to remove the starchy taste of the raw flour. Gradually beat in the stock and cream. Increase heat to medium and continue beating with the wire whisk until the sauce reaches the boiling point and thickens. Season with salt and pepper to taste.

Arrange the chicken on a heated platter. Spoon some of the sauce over the chicken, or pour into a sauceboat and pass separately.

Serve with mashed potatoes and a buttered green vegetable, and a light red wine with a somewhat fruity bouquet, as this is a fairly delicate dish. My suggestion would be one of the lighter-bodied California Petit Sirahs or Zinfandels.

Makes 4 to 6 servings.

CHICKEN IN BRIOCHE

———————— ❖❖❖ ————————

This elegant French dish is not nearly so difficult to prepare as one might suspect. And the taste combination of the chicken and brioche is rich, buttery, and heavenly.

1 *recipe brioche dough (see below)*	1 *teaspoon salt*
4 *Tablespoons butter*	½ *teaspoon freshly ground black pepper*
Legs, breasts (split in half), and thighs of 2 2½- to 3-pound fryers (1¼–1½ kilograms)	*Flour, for rolling out the pastry*
	1 *egg yolk, beaten*

The day before preparing this recipe, make a batch of brioche dough from your favorite recipe. Any recipe using a minimum of about 3½ cups of flour is fine. There is a long, carefully detailed recipe in Volume 2 of *Mastering the Art of French Cooking* by Julia Child and Simone Beck for brioche dough prepared in the traditional French manner. There is a less orthodox recipe for a brioche loaf using melted butter in James Beard's *Beard on Bread,* and an easy recipe using frozen butter in the recipe booklet that accompanies the Cuisinart ™ Food Processor. If making the food-processor brioche dough, you will have to make two batches, as the recipe only calls for 2 cups of flour.

Refrigerate overnight.

Preheat oven to 475° F.

Melt the buttter in a large skillet over medium-low heat. When the foam subsides, add the chicken, 3 or 4 pieces at a time, skin side down. Sauté gently, turning often, for 5 or 6 minutes until the chicken has "plumped" and the flesh becomes white. The chicken should take on only the lightest golden hue. Lower the heat, if necessary, to prevent browning.

When all the chicken has been sautéed, generously rub a large baking sheet with the butter from the skillet.

Pat the chicken thoroughly dry. Season with salt and pepper. Cut the brioche dough in half. Return half to the refrigerator. Quickly shape the dough into a disc. Place on a lightly floured surface, and roll it out into a thin sheet, ⅛ to ¼ inch thick. The dough will seem stiff and difficult to roll at first, but will roll out easily as it begins to get thinner.

Think of the dough as a piece of wrapping paper. Cut out a piece that looks large enough to wrap one of the pieces of chicken. Brush off any excess flour, and place the chicken on the piece of brioche, skin side down. Wrap the dough around the chicken, folding in the edges as you would a package. Bring the brioche together into a long if slightly irregular seam, and pinch firmly together. If you have cut too large a piece of dough, trim the excess before pressing together at the seam. Place seam side down on the buttered baking sheet. Repeat with the remaining pieces, rolling out the second piece of dough when the first is used up.

Brush the chicken with the beaten egg yolk, brushing as far down the sides as you can. Make a small hole in the top of each piece to allow the steam to escape.

Place in the 475° F. oven and bake 5 minutes. Reduce heat to 375° F. and bake 15 to 20 minutes longer.

Serve immediately with a white sauce made from chicken broth and cream, and enriched with egg yolks (see page 203). Serve with young green beans poached in butter, or fresh young peas, pearl onions, and button mushrooms flavored with fresh tarragon.

An elegant white Burgundy would be lovely, something in the Montrachet family such as a Chassagne-Montrachet or a Chevalier-Montrachet. If you prefer a red wine, it should be an equally lovely one, also from Burgundy, such as a Fixin or a Chambertin-Clos de Bèze.

If you plan 1 piece of chicken in brioche per person, this recipe will serve 12. It can easily be halved by using less chicken and baking the leftover brioche as a bread.

6

OTHER
PREPARATIONS

THE FIRST FIVE CHAPTERS of this book have dealt with the most important and basic techniques of American cooking—roasting, broiling, and grilling; and the various ways of cooking by moist heat, sautéing, frying, and baking. This chapter includes other methods of preparation which do not easily fit into the preceding categories. There are terrines and mousses, and some salads and sandwiches, but there is also a paella, a bright and festive Spanish dish that is a cross between steamed and poached. There's a tea-leaf-smoked chicken, which is based on a recipe from *The New York Times*, and there's even a recipe for chicken and seafood sausages.

TEA-LEAF-SMOKED CHICKEN

This is an easy and exciting recipe to cook. The beautiful flavor is so unlike chicken smoked with hickory or apple wood. But there are a few words of caution: During the 10 minutes of smoking, keep a window open and the kitchen door closed because the smoke will bellow from the pot. And be sure to let the chicken cool at least to room temperature before eating it, so that it can take on its full flavor.

This smoked chicken can be used as an hors d'oeuvre, cut into small pieces and served at room temperature, or it can be made ahead of time and served as a main course for lunch. Serve it on a bed of lettuce, garnished with a few sprigs of parsley or watercress, or with a salad.

¼ cup soy sauce	Boiling water
1 Tablespoon ground ginger	½ cup flour
2 Tablespoons black pepper-	½ cup sugar
corns, coarsely ground	½ cup Assam or Lapsong
1 teaspoon cayenne	Souchong tea leaves (25
1 teaspoon cinnamon	grams)
1 2½- to 3-pound chicken	¼ cup sesame oil
(1¼–1½ kilograms)	

Combine the soy sauce, ginger, pepper, cayenne, and cinnamon. Rub well onto the chicken, inside and outside, pressing the pepper into the skin. Truss (see page 221). Allow to marinate at room temperature for 3 hours.

Place the chicken in a large pot. Add enough boiling water to cover, and place over medium-high heat. When the liquid comes back to a boil, reduce heat and simmer for 45 to 50 minutes, or until the internal temperature of the thickest part of the thigh registers 165° F. on an instantly registering thermometer.

Remove, and cool the chicken on a rack at room temperature for 20 minutes.

Line the bottom of a large, heavy pot with a single layer of aluminum foil. Combine the flour and sugar and spread *evenly* over the foil. Sprinkle the tea leaves evenly across the sugar and flour mixture. Place a rack over the tea. Set the pot over medium-high heat. When the tea begins to smoke, place the chicken on its side on the rack. Cover, reduce heat to medium, and smoke 6 to 8 minutes. Turn the chicken onto its other side, and smoke another 6 to 8 minutes.

Remove the chicken and cool at room temperature for a few minutes, then rub with oil.

Serve at room temperature. Makes 4 to 6 servings.

Any size chicken can be poached for this recipe (accurate poaching times can be found on page 62), and then smoked. Tiny birds need only about 4 minutes of smoking on each side; larger birds as much as 8 to 10 minutes.

I'd suggest serving one of Germany's finest white wines, a fruity, medium-bodied, extremely elegant Wehlener Sonnenuhr from the Moselle. Bernkasteler Doktor from the same area is better known in this country and easier to find and certainly would go well.

PAELLA

❖❖❖

Paella is a dish with tremendous regional variations in its native Spain. There are as many different paellas as there are different bouillabaises in France or southern fried chickens in this country. Properly cooked, it can be a magnificent party meal in itself—festive, colorful, delicious, and expensive.

Simply described, this paella is a saffron-rice salad with shrimp, lobster meat, chorizo (Spanish sausage), peas, green peppers, onions, tomatoes, and garlic, garnished with steamed mussels and clams, chicken, and lobster claws. But to get all of those ingredients into one dish without overcooking half of them, and undercooking the rest, requires that they be cooked in a special sequence. Paella is an excellent example of what might be called "additive cookery."

1½ pounds fresh peas, podded
  (1 kilogram)
1 1- to 1½-pound lobster (½
  kilogram)
1 quart mussels (1 liter)
12 to 15 clams
1 pound shrimp (500 grams)
⅓ cup oil
1 garlic clove, finely chopped
½ teaspoon oregano
1 teaspoon paprika
1 teaspoon salt
½ teaspoon freshly ground
  black pepper
1 2½- to 3-pound chicken, cut
  into serving pieces (see page
  224) (1¼–1½ kilograms)

4 Tablespoons oil
1 large onion, chopped
2 garlic cloves, finely chopped
1 green pepper, seeded and
  chopped
3 medium-sized tomatoes,
  peeled, seeded, and coarsely
  chopped
¼ pound chorizo (Spanish
  sausage), sliced (125 grams)
1 teaspoon salt
½ teaspoon freshly ground
  black pepper
2 cups rice
1 quart boiling chicken stock
  (1 liter)
1 teaspoon saffron

Cook the peas in boiling salted water until just tender, about 5 to 8 minutes. Drain, and cool completely under cold running water.

Place the lobster in a large pot of boiling salted water. When water returns to a boil, reduce heat and simmer for exactly 5 minutes. Drain and cool under cold running water. Remove the tail meat and dice in large pieces. Crack the claws and save for garnish.

Scrub the mussels and clams clean in cold water. Shell and devein the shrimp.

Combine the oil, garlic clove, oregano, paprika, salt, and pepper, and mix well. Brush generously on the chicken.

Heat the 4 tablespoons of oil in a large pot or paella pan over medium heat. Add the chicken, skin side down, 3 or 4 pieces at a time. Sauté quickly until golden brown, turning the chicken once or twice. Set aside. Add the onions and garlic to the pan, and sauté for 3 or 4 minutes over medium-high heat until golden brown, but not burnt. Reduce heat, and add the green pepper. Cook slowly for 5 minutes. Add the tomatoes and chorizo, and simmer for 5 minutes more. Add the salt and black pepper, and stir in the rice. Cook over medium heat for 2 or 3 minutes until rice becomes white and opaque. Stir in the boiling stock and saffron, and add the shrimp and chicken. Reduce heat, cover tightly, and simmer for 20 minutes, until the rice is tender and has absorbed all the liquid.

While rice is cooking, prepare the mussels and clams. Place each in a separate saucepan with ½ cup water. Cover, and place over medium-high heat for 6 to 8 minutes, or until opened. Remove and discard any clams or mussels that have not opened.

When the rice is tender, stir in the peas and lobster meat with a fork. Taste for seasoning; add more salt and pepper if necessary. Arrange the mussels, clams, and reserved lobster claws on the rice; cover, and simmer for 5 minutes longer. Serve immediately.

I suspect that at one time or another virtually every fish and crustacean from Neptune's basket has been a part of a paella— everything from snails and inkfish to bass and whiting. Sometimes fish stock is used in place of chicken stock, sometimes good olive oil. I sometimes steam the clams and mussels first, and combine their steaming liquids with enough chicken broth to make 1 quart of liquid. This adds a little more fish taste to the rice. Rice is a staple of Spain, and it is perhaps the only ingredient one can safely say *must* be in a paella, so feel free to make your paella with whatever ingredients are available in your local markets.

Your choice of wine should follow your choice of ingredients in the paella. If you're using primarily chicken and sausages, I'd recommend a red Rioja wine of northern Spain. If, on the other hand, you are concentrating on seafoods, a crisp, Spanish dry white wine would be lovely.

Makes 10 to 12 servings.

FARMHOUSE TERRINE

――――――― ✦✦✦ ―――――――

This recipe produces an enormous terrine that is not only good to look at, but delicious to eat. Because of its size, it is perfect for large parties.

1 *pound shoulder of pork*
  (500 grams)
1 *pound shoulder of veal*
  (500 grams)
1 *pound ham* (500 grams)
1 *pound pork fat* (500 grams)
⅓ *cup* Cognac
⅓ *cup dry white wine*
¼ *teaspoon crushed dried bay*
  leaves
1 *teaspoon crushed dried*
  thyme
½ *teaspoon freshly grated*
  nutmeg
1½ *teaspoons salt*

1 *teaspoon freshly ground*
  black pepper
3 *Tablespoons rendered*
  chicken fat or oil
½ *medium onion, peeled and*
  finely chopped
3 *garlic cloves, peeled and*
  finely chopped
1 5- *to* 5½-*pound chicken*
  (2¼–2½ *kilograms*)
3 *eggs, well beaten*
⅛-*inch-thick sheets of fat*
  back or other pork fat to
  line the terrine

Dice ½ pound of the pork shoulder, ½ pound of the veal, ½ pound of the ham, and ½ pound of the pork fat into ¾-inch pieces. Combine the diced meats and fat in a very large bowl; add the Cognac, wine, bay leaves, thyme, nutmeg, salt, and pepper. Mix well. Pour the chicken fat or oil into a skillet over medium heat. When hot, add the onion and garlic and sauté until tender and translucent, about 3 minutes. Mix into the diced meats.

Preheat oven to 375° F.

With a sharp, sturdy knife, cut through the skin and fat of the chicken from stem to stern along the entire length of the backbone. Slide the point of your knife under one side of the cut to make a flap so that you can begin to peel the skin and meat away from the carcass. Using the edge of the knife, gradually separate the meat and the skin from the carcass, following the natural curves of the carcass, and cutting through the shoulder and thigh joints as they become exposed. When you have peeled half the carcass clean, turn the chicken around and repeat on the other side. Lift out the carcass and reserve for stock, or discard. Place the boneless bird on the counter, skin down. Remove the breast in 2 pieces and mix them into the diced meats. Cut off the wings and reserve for another use. Using your fingers, remove the legs and the thighs from the skin covering it without puncturing the skin. The skin should now be in one piece, flat on the counter. Toss the skin into the bowl, and mix with the terrine mixture.

Remove all of the meat from the legs and thighs, and combine it with the remaining pork shoulder, veal shoulder, ham, and pork fat. Chop very finely, either by hand or in a food processor, or grind once through the coarse blade of a meat grinder. Add to the terrine mixture, and mix well with your hands.

Form a couple of tablespoons of the mixture into a patty. Heat a little oil in a small skillet and sauté the patty until cooked through. Cool, then taste. Adjust the seasonings, adding more salt, pepper, nutmeg, or thyme as needed.

Remove the skin and the 2 large pieces of the breast. Add the beaten eggs, and mix until thoroughly combined.

Stretch the skin across the bottom of a large terrine, or any ovenproof mold that looks large enough to hold all of the mixed meats. Line the exposed walls of the terrine with sheets of pork fat, allowing the fat to drape over the edges of the mold. Spread about half the meat mixture into the terrine. Arrange the 2 pieces of breast in a line across the top of the meats, then cover with the remaining mixture. Fold the ends of the sheets of pork fat across the top of the terrine. Use additional fat if the entire top surface is not covered.

Seal the terrine tightly with a double layer of foil and cover. Place in a pan filled with hot water, and bake for 2½ to 2¾ hours. Cool to room temperature, or at least until the mold can be handled without burning yourself. Press a layer of foil into the mold so that the top of the terrine is protected. Fit a board or lid snugly on top of the terrine mixture, and place 8 to 10 pounds of miscellaneous weights on it—heavy canned products, kitchen weights, an old meat grinder, almost anything heavy can be used. Refrigerate overnight.

To unmold, run a knife around the edge of the terrine. Fill the sink with very hot water, and plunge the bottom of the terrine into the water for about 20 seconds. Invert over a large platter, tray, or carving board, rapping it sharply against a secure counter if it doesn't drop out immediately. Slide your fingers around the terrine to remove the jelly which has clung to the outside. The jelly isn't very attractive, but it is delicious and should be served. Serve the terrine at room temperature.

This terrine would be excellent with any number of dry white wines from France, Italy, or California. In particular, I would recommend either a Pouilly-Fuissé, a Chablis, an Orvieto, or a California Chardonnay.

Makes enough to serve 30 to 40 at a cocktail party.

CHICKEN AND SALMON SAUSAGES

❖❖❖

This is an exciting appetizer for an elegant dinner. It is relatively easy to make if you own a food processor and can obtain some sausage casings from a butcher. It has a soft, delicate taste and is best served without garnish on a plate that has been filmed with a rich white sauce or sauce Nantua (see page 110).

¾ *pound raw chicken* (350 grams)
1 *whole egg plus* 1 *egg white*
Salt
Pepper
Paprika
4 *to* 5 *drops Tabasco sauce*
⅔ *cup heavy cream*

¼ *cup chopped parsley*
⅓ *cup finely chopped mushrooms*
⅓ *cup finely chopped raw salmon*
Sausage casings
3 *Tablespoons oil*

In a food processor fitted with the metal blade, combine the chicken, egg and egg white, a little salt, pepper, paprika, and the Tabasco. Purée until very smooth, about 20 seconds. With the food processor still puréeing, gradually pour in the cream. Taste, and add more salt and pepper if necessary.

Transfer the mixture to a large bowl, and stir in the parsley, mushrooms, and salmon.

Rinse the sausage casings under cold running water and slide onto the nozzle of a sausage stuffer. With a small piece of string, tie off the end. Stuff the casings loosely with the sausage mixture, and tie into links about 3 inches long. With the point of a skewer or small knife, prick each sausage in 3 or 4 places.

Add the string of sausages to boiling salted water. Reduce the heat, and simmer very gently, uncovered, for 1 hour. Cool the sausages slightly under cold running water. Pat thoroughly dry.

Pour 3 tablespoons of oil into a large skillet over medium-high heat. When very hot, add the sausages and sauté until lightly browned on each side. This final browning breaks down the casings, which would otherwise taste rubbery and be difficult to chew. Serve immediately on plates filmed generously with a rich white sauce or a sauce Nantua.

Makes about 8 sausages.

I'd probably serve a medium-bodied white wine with some fruit, such as a Vouvray from the Loire Valley in France, unless this dish were served with a sauce Nantua, in which case I would prefer a "bigger" wine with more oak-barrel aging, such as a truly fine California Chardonnay.

CHICKENBURGERS WITH HAM AND BLACK OLIVES

———— ❖❖❖ ————

These colorful patties have a hearty flavor that is a welcome alternative to hamburgers.

2 *Tablespoons butter*
½ *medium onion, finely chopped*
1 *garlic clove, finely chopped*
¾ *cup fresh white bread crumbs*
8 *to* 10 *ounces raw chicken, finely ground (250–300 grams)*
¼ *cup finely diced ham*
3 *or* 4 *black olives, pitted and finely chopped*

1 *egg white*
1 *Tablespoon chopped fresh basil, or* 1 *teaspoon crushed dried basil*
1 *teaspoon salt*
½ *teaspoon freshly ground black pepper*
Flour
3 *to* 4 *Tablespoons oil*

Melt the butter in a small skillet over medium heat. When hot, add the onion and garlic. Sauté until tender and translucent, about 3 minutes.

In a mixing bowl, combine the sautéed onions with the bread crumbs, ground chicken, ham, black olives, egg white, basil, salt, and pepper. Mix well.

Shape into patties, about 2 inches in diameter. Roll lightly in flour and pat off any excess.

Pour the oil into a large skillet over medium heat. When hot, add the patties. Sauté for 5 to 6 minutes, turning occasionally until the patties are evenly colored to a golden brown. Sauté in 2 batches if necessary.

Serve on hamburger buns, or with a tomato sauce. When served without the tomato sauce, I'd recommend a fairly fruity rosé, either a Tavel from France or a California rosé of Cabernet Sauvignon, which has the bouquet of a French Cabernet Sauvignon but is a lighter wine. If chickenburgers are to be served with ketchup, stick to beer, as the spices in this condiment do nothing to enhance the flavor of any wine.

Makes 8 patties.

HERBED CHICKEN MOUSSE

——— ❖❖❖ ———

This mousse is easy to prepare, but it does require a food processor. It looks beautiful on a plate, with the cream-colored chicken all speckled with fresh herbs and the line of ham running through the center. It is equally good served hot with a hollandaise or mousseline sauce or cold with a gently flavored lemon mayonnaise.

8 ounces raw chicken (250 grams)
2 egg whites
⅛ teaspoon mace
⅛ teaspoon cayenne
1 teaspoon salt
½ teaspoon freshly ground black pepper
½ cup sour cream
½ cup chopped parsley
¼ cup chopped chives
1 Tablespoon chopped fresh tarragon, or 1 teaspoon crushed, dried tarragon
½ cup heavy cream, beaten until it holds a soft peak
3 to 4 thick slices ham

Preheat oven to 350° F.

Combine the raw chicken, egg whites, mace, cayenne, salt, and pepper in a food processor. Purée until very smooth, about 20 seconds. Add the sour cream, parsley, chives, and tarragon, and process 10 seconds. Transfer to a large bowl, and fold in the whipped cream.

Spread half the mixture on the bottom of a small, well-buttered terrine or ovenproof dish. Arrange the sliced ham in a layer on top of the chicken mixture. Spread the remaining chicken mixture in a layer over the ham. Rinse your hand under cold running water, then use your fingers to smoothe the mixture on the top of the terrine. Cover the terrine with a double layer of aluminum foil, and place in a large pan filled with hot water. The water should come most of the way up the sides of the terrine.

Place in the oven, and bake for 60 minutes. Unmold and serve hot or cold as an hors d'oeuvre.

Serve with a white wine with a "crisp" backbone—that is,

with enough acidity to tingle in the mouth for several seconds after you've swallowed it. A good match would be a Muscadet from France's Loire Valley or a Frascati from Italy.

NOTES ON LEFTOVERS AND SERVING COLD CHICKEN

❖❖❖

One of the best things about cooking chicken is that there are often leftovers, and sometimes I deliberately cook more than I need so I will be assured of a nice supply of leftover chicken. Probably the simplest use of leftover cooked chicken is to serve it cold with one of the sauces suggested in Chapter 9. Cold chicken should be stored and served at room temperature, if possible, and ideally should be from a poached chicken. A flavored mayonnaise is always great with cold chicken, but there is a lavishly rich alternative—a cold hollandaise, suggested on page 212. The green sauce on page 214 is also excellent. Cold chicken placed on a leaf or two of lettuce with alternating slices of tomato and sweet onion arranged next to it, and a dollop of sauce on the side, makes a quick, easy, and delicious lunch.

There are a number of recipes in this chapter that call for cooked chicken, all of which can be used with leftovers. But there is a veritable barrage of other possibilities. Cooked chicken can be mixed with other vegetables, perhaps some eggs or cream, and made into a hash. It can be moistened with a white sauce and used as a filling for crêpes or omelettes. It can be added to a custard and baked into a quiche. Stir some finely diced chicken into your next cheese soufflé, and add a ¼ cup of chopped chives or scallions with it. It can be used for a tetrazzini, a divan, a pilaf, or mixed with sweetbreads and mushrooms as a stuffing for *vol-au-vents*. Or used in salads and sandwiches.

CHICKEN CROQUETTES

———— ❖❖❖ ————

Using cheese as a base is a simple and delicious way to make croquettes.

2 cups finely diced cooked
  chicken
½ cup ricotta cheese (125
  grams)
2 Tablespoons grated Par-
  mesan cheese
½ cup mixed fresh herbs
  (parsley, chives, and tarragon make an excellent
  combination here)

½ teaspoon salt
¼ teaspoon freshly ground
  black pepper
½ cup flour
1 egg, well beaten
½ cup dry bread crumbs
2 Tablespoons butter
2 Tablespoons oil

Combine the chicken, cheeses, herbs, salt, and pepper, and mix thoroughly until all the ingredients bind together and form a large, firm mass. Taste a small amount, and adjust the seasoning.

Arrange the flour on a plate with the beaten egg in a bowl next to it, and the bread crumbs next to that. Form the mixture into 6 croquettes (patties), about 2 inches in diameter. Coat each croquette lightly in flour, dip into the beaten egg, then roll in bread crumbs.

Place the butter and oil in a skillet over medium heat. When hot, add the croquettes and sauté until golden brown, about 2 minutes on each side.

Serve at once with tomato sauce, and with a round, soft white wine such as a Sylvaner from Alsace, or with a California Blanc de Blancs.

COLD CURRIED CHICKEN
OR HOT DEVILED CHICKEN

————— ❖❖❖ —————

This dish is as good hot as it is cold, and it's a terrific way to use up leftover cooked chicken.

16 *ounces natural, flavored*   ½ *teaspoon freshly ground*
    yogurt (500 grams)   *black pepper*
½ *cup oil*   1 *teaspoon Dijon mustard*
2 *Tablespoons curry powder*   4 *to 6 cups cooked chicken*
1 *teaspoon salt*

FOR DEVILING

½ *cup toasted sesame seeds*
    (75 grams)

Combine the yogurt, oil, curry powder, salt, pepper, and mustard, and mix thoroughly. Taste, and adjust the seasonings. Add the chicken, mix well, and serve either slightly chilled or at room temperature.

For hot deviled chicken, place the curried chicken in an oven-proof dish, top with toasted sesame seeds, and cover with foil. Heat in a 375° F. oven until bubbling hot, about 25 to 30 minutes. Serve with rice or noodles.

Hot or cold, this type of spicy dish marries best with a "spicy" wine—that is, a wine with an almost pungent, powerful bouquet. In this case, a Gewürztraminer from Alsace or from California would be perfect.

Makes 6 to 8 servings.

CHICKEN SALADS

❖❖❖

There are two chicken salad recipes in this book—one with an oil and vinegar dressing and one with a mayonnaise dressing. They are two of my favorite chicken salads, both distinct and delicious. They don't even begin to give you an idea of the variety possible in chicken salads. There's the traditional chicken and celery salad dressed with mayonnaise. For an elegant lunch you could mix very finely diced chicken with a mayonnaise flavored with chives or scallion or onion, capers, and lemon juice, and then roll in long, thin slices of smoked salmon, place on a bed of soft green lettuce leaves and garnish with a wedge of lemon. Chicken and cooked cauliflower are also delicious together, mixed with a Russian or Thousand Island dressing. Or you might make a salad of chicken and mushrooms and serve it stuffed into either avocados or tomatoes. Chicken salad is a good way to use up leftovers, and a great place to be creative.

CHICKEN SALAD
WITH BROCCOLI

❖❖❖

This is an incredibly beautiful salad with a light, refreshing taste. It is an excellent alternative to serving salade Niçoise, especially if presented on a bed of soft green lettuce and decoratively garnished with a few small, wrinkly, jet-black imported olives.

2 *small bunches broccoli*
¼ *cup parsley, chopped*
¼ *cup fresh tarragon, chopped*
¼ *pound mushrooms, sliced (125 grams)*

3 *small tomatoes, cut into wedges*
1 *cup cooked chicken, diced*
½ *small onion, finely chopped*
Vinaigrette dressing (see page 213)

Remove the leaves from the broccoli stems and chop with the parsley and tarragon. Cut the broccoli into small pieces, or flowerettes. Chop and reserve the leaves; discard the stems. Cook in boiling salted water for 4 to 5 minutes, until tender but slightly crunchy. Immediately place under cold running water until completely cooled. Drain on paper toweling.

In a large bowl, combine the broccoli, mushrooms, tomatoes, chicken and onion. Add the parsley, tarragon, and chopped broccoli leaves.

Prepare a basic vinaigrette sauce, using a lemon, good olive oil, salt, and lots of coarsely ground black pepper.

Pour dressing over the salad and toss gently.

It's frequently said that no wine marries well with a vinegar-based salad dressing. Perhaps because of my Italian upbringing I believe the opposite is true—that practically all salads should be accompanied by wine. Just remember, before taking a sip of wine, to eat a bite of something solid, such as the chicken, which won't have absorbed too much dressing. Having said this, I would stick to the Italian tradition and serve a Frascati from the Roman Hills or an Est Est Est from Montefiascone.

CHICKEN SALAD
WITH SOUR CREAM DRESSING

❖❖❖

4 *to 5 cups cooked chicken, diced*	½ *celery rib, finely chopped*
¾ *cup walnuts, coarsely chopped*	½ *cup chopped parsley*
	½ *small onion, finely chopped*
2 *Tablespoons capers*	*Salt*
⅓ *cup sliced black olives*	*Freshly ground black pepper*

DRESSING

¾ *cup mayonnaise (see page 207)*	3 *Tablespoons Dijon mustard*
½ *cup commercial sour cream (125 grams)*	*Salt*
	Freshly ground black pepper

In a large bowl, combine the chicken, walnuts, capers, olives, celery, parsley, and onion. Mix well, and season with salt and pepper.

In a separate bowl, combine the mayonnaise, sour cream, and mustard. Taste, add more mustard if you wish, and season with salt and pepper.

Combine the salad with enough dressing to loosely bind it together. Taste for seasoning.

Arrange on a bed of lettuce, and garnish with additional black olives. Serve with a well-chilled white wine with a certain amount of crispness such as a Pouilly-Fumé of France's Loire Valley or a Fumé Blanc from California.

CHICKEN IN LETTUCE LEAVES

———— ❖❖❖ ————

This is a Chinese way of serving poultry—the chicken is finely diced, mixed with vegetables, seasonings, toasted almonds, and served hot, passed with a plate of very cold lettuce leaves. Each person spoons some of the chicken mixture into a lettuce leaf and rolls it up. The different textures and tastes in this recipe, as well as the hot-cold contrast of the chicken and the lettuce, make it both unusual and delicious.

6 *Tablespoons butter or oil*
2 *medium onions, finely chopped*
1 *green pepper, finely chopped*
1 *small hot pepper, finely chopped (optional)*
2 *cups cooked chicken, finely diced*
1 *cup cooked rice*
2 *Tablespoons chopped fresh basil or 1½ teaspoons crushed dried basil*

¼ *cup chicken stock*
¼ *cup Cognac*
Salt
Freshly ground black pepper
¼ *cup chopped parsley*
¾ *cup toasted almonds, coarsely chopped*
Iceberg lettuce leaves, well chilled

Heat the butter or oil in a large skillet over medium heat. When hot, add the onion, green pepper, and hot pepper. Sauté for 5 to 6 minutes. Add the chicken, rice, basil, stock, and Cognac. Mix well, cover, and simmer for 2 to 3 minutes. Taste, and season with salt and pepper. Cover, and cook for another minute or two until very hot. Arrange on a heated platter, and garnish with the chopped parsley and toasted almonds. Serve with lettuce leaves.

Many medium-bodied white wines would go well with this dish, such as an Orvieto Abbocato from Italy, a Gewürztraminer from California, or a Vouvray from France.

Makes 6 to 8 servings.

MININA

———— ❖❖❖ ————

This is a Middle Eastern version of an Italian *frittata*. It is made with cooked chicken, hard-boiled eggs, calves' brains, and fresh herbs. After baking, it is enriched with chicken stock, unmolded, cut into wedges, and garnished with lemon.

½ pound calves' brains (250 grams)	*9 eggs, beaten together*
Salt	*¼ cup chopped parsley*
Juice of ½ large lemon	*¼ cup chopped fresh tarragon*
1 cup cooked chicken, diced	*Freshly ground black pepper*
3 hard-boiled eggs, finely chopped	*4 Tablespoons oil*
	¼ cup rich chicken stock
	Lemon wedges

Soak the brains in cold water for 1 hour.

Preheat oven to 350° F.

Carefully clean the brains, removing the outer membrane and trimming around the base. Rinse under cold running water. Place the brains in a saucepan with 6 cups of cold water, a little salt, and the lemon juice. Bring to just under a rolling boil over medium-high heat, then reduce the heat and simmer for 5 minutes. Drain, pat dry, and dice.

Combine the brains, chicken, and hard-boiled eggs in a large bowl with the beaten eggs, parsley, and tarragon. Season with salt and pepper.

Heat the oil in an ovenproof skillet or baking dish. When very hot, pour in the egg mixture. Cook for 1 to 2 minutes on the burner so that the bottom sets. Transfer to the oven, and bake for 20 to 25 minutes, or until a knife inserted in the center comes out clean. Spoon the stock over the baked eggs, loosen around the edges with a knife, and invert onto a warm serving plate. Cut into wedges and garnish with lemon.

This is a good brunch dish, if your guests aren't squeamish about eating brains. It also makes a lovely, light luncheon recipe or a good first course.

Serve with a light, appealing white wine such as a Verdicchio from Italy, or, for a wine "born" closer to this dish's geographic origins, try a dry white, St. Helena, the wine of Greece's Peloponnesian peninsula.

Makes 6 to 8 servings.

CROQUE MADAME (CRUNCHY LADY)

❖❖❖

Wife of the famous French *croque monsieur*—the ham and cheese sandwich of Parisian cafés—*madame* is plumper than *monsieur*, for she includes chicken as well as ham and cheese. It is a sandwich that can conjure up delicious memories of café life in Paris, of passing hours and passing people. Properly made with a creamy Gruyère, thin slices of a good country ham, moist pieces of freshly cooked chicken, and copious quantities of sweet butter, it is an outstanding meal, served with a salad, or perhaps a bowl of hot soup.

Butter
Bread, preferably homemade,
*   crust removed and sliced*
Mustard, preferably from
*   Dijon or Meaux*

Swiss cheese, preferably a
*   Gruyère, thinly sliced*
Ham, preferably a good
*   country ham, thinly sliced*
Cooked chicken

There are special *croque monsieur* grills which press the sandwich into a scallop shape. But the sandwich can also be made on waffle irons or electric grills.

Generously butter 2 slices of bread. Spread a little mustard across the other side of each slice. Arrange a slice of cheese, a slice of ham, and a few pieces of chicken on the mustard-coated side. Top with the other slice of bread, and grill in a *croque monsieur* grill or waffle iron. The sandwich should be cooked for 3 to 4 minutes on each side over medium-high heat, or for 3 to 4 minutes if both sides are heated at once.

The sandwich can be fried in butter, if you wish, rather than grilled. A nice variation for brunch is to dip the bread in beaten eggs (as you would French toast), then fry.

Perfect with any number of fruity rosé wines or with round white wines such as California Chénin Blanc or German Liebfraumilch, this dish will also go well with everything from Campari and soda to Bloody Marys when served as brunch.

INSTANT CHICKEN PIE

❖❖❖

There are an incredible number of different chicken pies and chicken pot pies. A chicken pot pie can be made from an old hen no longer good for laying eggs, or it can be an elegant combination of a young and specially poached bird combined with freshly shucked oysters and baked in a delicately seasoned white wine sauce. The one element that all these share in common is a crust. Traditionally there was a bottom as well as a top crust, but as our aesthetics have begun to demand crispness in crusts, the saturated soggy bottom crust has disappeared.

An instant chicken pie is any combination of vegetables and chicken, or chicken and seafood, moistened with a white sauce, and topped just before serving with a piece of crust which has been baked separately and ahead of time. As a matter of fact, everything is prepared ahead of time—the white sauce, the vegetables, the chicken, whatever, and then just before serving, the whole is combined and reheated, and then a piece of crust laid on top as it is served. It can be made with leftover vegetables and chicken, or with a special combination of ingredients purchased specifically for the pie. And the "top" crust is so crisp your family or guests will be amazed.

INGREDIENTS

VEGETABLES: All the vegetables should be precooked, either by boiling until just tender and then cooling and refreshing them in cold water or, in the case of mushrooms, by sautéing in butter for 2 to 3 minutes. Pearl onions, potatoes, carrots, and celery are good, though green beans, asparagus tips, peas, button mushrooms, and even chestnuts can be used. Once the vegetable or combination of vegetables has been cooked and cooled they should be covered and stored at room temperature until you are ready to combine them with the chicken and sauce for reheating. Some chopped fresh herbs are great in this pie—parsley, chives, tarragon, or if you grow your own, perhaps some lemon thyme and rosemary.

CHICKEN: I am most comfortable when the pie is about one third chicken, so if you are using leftover chicken, plan to use twice as much in vegetables. If you are cooking a chicken specifically for a pie, poaching gives the best texture. The chicken can be diced in largish pieces (smaller pieces if you are using this recipe to stretch leftovers), or cut in pieces separated along the natural muscle planes.

SEAFOOD: Shellfish go beautifully with chicken, especially shrimp, crawfish tails, lobster meat, oysters, and mussels. With the exception of oysters, which only need the gentlest warming through, the shellfish should be precooked and shelled. Larger pieces of meat, perhaps from a lobster tail, can be diced.

THE SAUCE: Any of the basic white sauces can be used. For 4 to 5 cups of cooked ingredients, a single recipe from Chapter 9, pages 201–205, should be sufficient. For larger quantities of Instant Pie, make a double recipe. The specific white sauce you make will depend on the ingredients you are using. With chicken and seafood, perhaps you'd make a sauce with part fish stock, chicken stock, or white wine; with simple leftover chicken and a few odd vegetables from the refrigerator, the sauce would be made with stock, or perhaps some stock and milk. Once the sauce has been made, cover it with a buttered round of waxed paper or plastic wrap to prevent a skin from forming, and store it at room temperature until needed.

THE CRUST: I like to use a small piece of leftover puff paste or rough puff paste.

Preheat oven to 425° F.

On a lightly floured board, roll about 4 ounces of puff paste into a rectangle ⅛ inch thick. Prick it all over with a kitchen fork, with no set of tine marks more than about half an inch from the ones above. This is to prevent it from rising. With a damp cloth, lightly moisten the bottom of a baking sheet. Transfer the puff paste to the baking sheet, top with a buttered baking sheet, and refrigerate for 15 to 20 minutes. Place in the preheated oven, reduce the heat to 350° F., and bake until lightly and evenly colored, about half an hour. Cool on a rack at room temperature. If you wish to reheat the crust, return it to a 400° F. oven for 6 to 8 minutes before serving.

ASSEMBLY

Uncover the sauce and bring it to a boil over medium to medium-high heat, stirring occasionally to prevent scorching. When the sauce reaches a boil, add the meat, fish, and vegetables and cook until thoroughly heated through, about 6 to 8 minutes. (The crust will reheat in a 400° F. oven in the same amount of time, should you wish it to be hot.) Taste the filling mixture, and adjust the seasonings, or stir in a few tablespoons of fresh herbs.

To serve, place the filling mixture on individual plates, and top with a piece of crust. The crust will cut easily with a long, serrated knife. Garnish with a few sprigs of watercress or parsley, or perhaps dill if you are using shellfish, and serve immediately.

If you're using a preponderance of seafood and delicate vegetables, serve with a dry white wine such as a Chablis. But if you're using more chicken and making this a gutsier dish, serve with a full-bodied red wine such as Châteauneuf-du-Pape from France or a California Zinfandel.

7

INNARDS
AND OTHER
LESS-USED
PARTS

THE VAST WEALTH of edible parts to a chicken, beside the main carcass, have unfortunately disappeared from most of our markets—because of a lack of demand, the expense of producing them, or because of federal health restrictions. Chicken livers are readily available and can be found fresh or frozen in most markets. Necks, hearts, and gizzards are more difficult to find, but at least they are still being processed in certain parts of the country. Unborn eggs, cockscombs, feet, kidneys, and testicles, each for their own reasons, have virtually disappeared.

Chicken livers are undeniably the most popular of all chicken innards. Relatively inexpensive and more versatile than any other organ meats, they can be sautéed, fried, broiled, or grilled. They can be made into dumplings, mousses, terrines, pâtés, spreads, and pastes. They can be used to flavor stuffings, omelettes, crêpes, risottos, and sauces. There is even a recipe in this chapter for knishes, a meat pie filled with liver, beef, and buckwheat groats.

As for extra chicken skins, there are a number of interesting ways to prepare them. Skins can be marinated and broiled or grilled, as in Japanese cooking, or cut into diamond shapes and fried, producing a crackling that is a great alternative to bowls of nuts at cocktail parties.

The hearts and gizzards make flavorful stock and soups, and are also good fricasseed and in salads. A gizzard, incidentally, is a bird's second stomach, which is used for grinding the hard bits of grain that are so much a part of the chicken's diet. The necks are good for making stock and soups, but not much else.

CHICKEN LIVERS

❖❖❖

Whenever possible, insist on fresh livers. Frozen livers lose their juices, the flavor becomes flat, and they develop a mealy texture. Chicken livers are very high in nutritional value, can be prepared in a multitude of exciting ways, and are relatively inexpensive—definitely one of the best buys in the supermarket today.

To CLEAN LIVERS: Pick over the livers, removing any connecting tissue or dried blood, and cutting off any dark-green or blackish discolorations. With a sharp knife, cut the livers into their two natural halves. Pat dry.

CHOPPED LIVER
(especially for Ken Krakower)

❖❖❖

This is my favorite kind of chopped liver, perhaps because it is the one I can remember my grandmother making once a week for the Sabbath meal. The onions are browned in chicken fat, then sautéed with the livers, and finally chopped with hard-boiled eggs. The taste is warm and hearty, and the texture perfect. Ken Krakower arrived just as I was testing this recipe and explained that in Philadelphia, where he now lives, "They don't know how to make chopped liver. They make it with mayonnaise." Heaven forbid!

8 *Tablespoons rendered chicken fat, or oil*
2 *medium onions, finely chopped*
1 *pound fresh chicken livers, cleaned (above) (500 grams)*

2 *hard-boiled eggs*
Salt
Freshly ground black pepper

Melt the chicken fat over medium-high heat in a large skillet. When hot, add the onions, and sauté until the edges of the onions begin to brown, about 4 minutes. Add the livers, reduce the heat to medium, and sauté with the onions until done, about 3 minutes, turning the livers often so that they color evenly as they cook. Be careful not to overcook the livers. When done, they should still be slightly pink inside.

Traditionally the chopping takes place in a large, oval chopping bowl with a curved chopping blade, but it can be done just as well on a large wooden board and with a cook's knife. Chop the liver and onions with the hard-boiled eggs. It should be chopped very finely, but not so much that it becomes pastelike. Taste, and season with salt and pepper. Cover tightly and refrigerate overnight.

You may wonder if there is really a perfect wine for chopped liver. Easy suggestions come from Israel, even if the chopped liver isn't to grace the Sabbath table. So a Sauvignon Blanc from Israel is certainly more than acceptable and appropriate if you're either Orthodox or feeling very Jewish. Otherwise, a combination I find extremely flattering to both the chicken livers and the wine is a hearty, robust, assertive wine, a fine, extremely dry and chilled Fino Sherry from Jerez in Spain—which is as much an acquired taste as is the chopped liver.

Makes 6 servings.

CHICKEN LIVER SAUTÉ
WITH BROWN SAUCE AND RICE

————— ❖❖❖ —————

This is a simple, straightforward dish that is easy to prepare. The livers are sautéed with onion and mushrooms, moistened with a little brown sauce, flavored with Madeira, if you wish, and then heaped on top of steaming rice. It makes a quick meal in itself for lunch, or a light supper.

4 *Tablespoons chicken fat, butter or oil*
1 *large onion, finely chopped*
2 *garlic cloves, finely chopped*
½ *pound mushrooms, sliced* (250 grams)
1½ *pounds fresh chicken livers, cleaned (see page 166) (750 grams)*

1 *cup Basic Brown Sauce (see page 216)*
¼ *cup Madeira, optional*
Salt
Freshly ground black pepper
Rice cooked in chicken stock
Chopped parsley for garnish

Melt the chicken fat or butter in a large skillet over medium heat. Add the onion, garlic and mushrooms, and sauté until the onions are translucent and the mushrooms cooked through, about 3 minutes. Add the livers, and sauté for another 2 to 3 minutes until evenly colored on all sides but still slightly pink inside. Add the brown sauce and Madeira, and cook for a minute or two until the sauce is bubbling hot.

Season with salt and pepper to taste.

Spoon the livers over cooked rice, sprinkle with chopped parsley, and serve immediately.

Again, I would serve this with a Spanish Fino Sherry, as recommended for Chopped Liver, or, if you prefer a touch of sweetness, serve with a slightly sweeter Sherry such as Amontillado, also from Spain's Jerez region.

Makes 6 to 8 servings.

CHICKEN LIVER FILLING

———— ❖❖❖ ————

This basic filling can be used for omelettes, crêpes, risotto, or pasta.

BASIC FILLING MIXTURE

3 *Tablespoons chicken fat or*   1 *pound fresh chicken livers,*
  butter   *cleaned (see page 166)*
1 *medium onion, finely*   *(500 grams)*
  chopped   *Salt*
1 *shallot, finely chopped*   *Freshly ground black pepper*
2 *garlic cloves, finely chopped*

Melt the chicken fat or butter in a large skillet over medium heat. When hot, add the onion, shallot, and garlic. Sauté until tender and translucent, about 3 minutes. Add the chicken livers, and sauté for 2 to 3 minutes, stirring and turning the livers until they color evenly on all sides and are still slightly pink inside. Season with salt and pepper. Scrape the livers and onions into a chopping bowl, or onto a large cutting board. Chop the livers coarsely, mixing them with the sautéed onion as you chop.

FOR OMELETTES

6 *Tablespoons melted butter*   *Chopped parsley for garnish*

Stir 4 tablespoons of butter into the warm filling, and spoon a few heaping tablespoons into each omelette. Brush the top of the omelettes with the remaining butter, and sprinkle with chopped parsley.

FOR CRÊPES

1 *cup Basic Brown Sauce*   *Chopped parsley for garnish*
  (see page 216)
2 *Tablespoons Sherry or*
  Madeira

Prepare the basic filling. Add ⅓ cup brown sauce and the Sherry or Madeira to the skillet in which the livers and onions were sautéed. Add the chopped livers to the sauce, and heat through. Spoon the filling into the crêpes and roll them. Coat the bottom of a gratin dish with a little sauce, and arrange the crêpes in it, seam side down. Top with the remaining brown sauce. Run under a broiler for a few minutes, or heat in a 400° F. oven until the sauce is bubbling. If you wish, a few sliced mushrooms can be added to the filling and sautéed with the onions and shallot. Sprinkle with chopped parsley and serve immediately.

Tomato sauce is a beautiful complement to livers, and this filling is delicious when tomato sauce is substituted for the brown sauce.

FOR RISOTTO

2 Tablespoons tomato purée   *2 Tablespoons Cognac*
or Tomato Sauce (see page
215)

Prepare a half recipe of the basic filling. When the livers are chopped, moisten them with the tomato purée and Cognac. Just before serving, stir into a risotto made from 1 cup rice and beef broth.

FOR PASTA

3 cups Tomato Sauce (see
page 215)

Prepare a half recipe of the basic filling. After chopping the livers, return them to the skillet and add the tomato sauce. As soon as the sauce is hot, pour over cooked noodles, spaghetti, or your favorite pasta. Serve immediately with grated Parmesan cheese, fresh bread and butter, and a salad.

In an omelette or crêpe, chances are you would serve this dish for either brunch or a light, elegant lunch, in which case I would accompany it with a crisp, dry white wine such as a Chablis or Pouilly-Fuissé.

Once you add tomato sauce and serve this "filling" on a risotto or spaghetti, I would suggest a bigger wine, a light to medium-bodied red wine such as a Valpolicella from Verona or a Merlot from Feiuli-Venezia-Giulia, both in northern Italy.

CHICKEN LIVER SPREAD

❖❖❖

This is a great spread for cocktail parties. The texture is soft and light, it spreads easily, and the liver taste is not overwhelming. I am one of the directors of The Society for More Spreadable Spreads. To me, there is nothing more frustrating and humiliating than the battle of the buffet table, the eternal fight to get some dense, heavy mixture off the knife and onto the cracker. And the final crushing blow to one's sense of humility, as I know all too well, is a handful of crumbled cracker crumbs. Fear not, this is one of the spreadable spreads.

I like to bake this spread in a 1-quart Pyrex mixing bowl. When it is inverted into a plate, it forms a simple, curved shape that needs little more garnish than a few sprigs of parsley or watercress laced around it. Beyond its serviceability as an hors d'oeuvre, it can be treated as a mousse or pâté, and it makes great sandwiches—with bacon or paper-thin slices of onion. It's also perfect for a quick lunch as an omelette filling.

3 *Tablespoons butter*	1 *teaspoon lemon juice*
½ *medium onion, chopped*	3 *to 4 drops Tabasco sauce*
2 *garlic cloves, finely chopped*	¼ *teaspoon salt*
½ *pound chicken livers,*	⅛ *teaspoon freshly ground*
cleaned (see page 166) (250	*black pepper*
grams)	*Fresh parsley or watercress*
2 *eggs*	*for garnish*
1 *cup heavy cream*	

Preheat the oven to 325° F.

Melt the butter in a skillet over medium heat. When hot, add the onion and garlic, and sauté for 3 to 4 minutes.

In a food processor or blender, combine the sautéed onion with all the remaining ingredients. Purée for 2 minutes. Pour through a strainer into a well-buttered 1-quart mold.

Place the mold in a deep pan of hot water. The water should come most of the way up the side of the mold. Bake for 1 hour to 1 hour and 15 minutes, or until a toothpick inserted into the center of the mold comes out clean.

When the liver has set, carefully remove from the water bath and cool to room temperature. Loosen the liver from the mold by running the tip of a knife around the edge. Invert onto a serving plate. Garnish with parsley or watercress. Accompany with crackers or Melba toast, rye or pumpernickel bread.

Assuming that you will be serving this nibble as a midday snack or before-dinner munch, I would recommend a jug of California Chablis, well chilled.

CHICKEN LIVER PÂTÉ

❖❖❖

1 *pound chicken livers,*
   cleaned (see page 166) (500
   grams)
3 *Tablespoons butter*
½ *medium onion*
2 *garlic cloves*

16 *Tablespoons softened*
   butter
2 *Tablespoons Cognac*
Dash of cayenne
Salt
Freshly ground black pepper

Add the livers to a large pan of boiling salted water. When the water comes back to the boil, reduce the heat and simmer for 10 minutes. Pour the cooked livers into a strainer, and cool completely under cold running water. Pat the livers dry.

While the livers are simmering, melt the butter in a skillet over medium-low heat. When hot, add the onion and garlic, and sauté until tender and translucent, about 3 minutes.

Purée the livers and onions in a food processor. Beat the purée into the softened butter. Add the Cognac, a big dash of cayenne, and overseason slightly with salt and pepper. Beat for a minute or two to be certain the seasonings are well distributed.

Pack into a lightly oiled mold, and chill in the refrigerator for at least 4 hours. Unmold, garnish with watercress or chopped parsley, and serve with bread or crackers. Almost any dry white wine or dry, Fino Sherry would be an appropriate accompaniment.

CHICKEN LIVERS RUMAKI, WITH WATER CHESTNUTS AND BACON

––––––––– ❖❖❖ –––––––––

This is a nice combination of textures and tastes. The spicy marinade brings out the flavor of the livers, and the chestnuts add a good contrast in texture and taste, with the bacon rounding it all off. It is a great hors d'oeuvre, or first course.

MARINADE

½ cup soy sauce
½ cup Worcestershire sauce
½ teaspoon freshly ground
  black pepper
1½ pounds chicken livers,
  cleaned and quartered (see
  page 166) (750 grams)

1 large can water chestnuts
½ pound bacon, cut in 1-inch
  pieces (250 grams)

Combine the soy, Worcestershire, and pepper, and mix well. Add the livers, and marinate for 2 to 4 hours.

Preheat a grill to very hot.

Arrange the bacon, chestnuts, and livers on bamboo skewers: bacon, liver, chestnut; bacon, liver, chestnut; and so on, beginning and ending with a piece of bacon.

Dip each skewer into the remaining marinade, and arrange on a grill, about 2 inches above the heat. Grill for 6 to 8 minutes, turning once or twice so that they cook and color evenly. Cut into a piece of liver in the center of one of the skewers. It should be slightly pink inside. If it still looks dark and raw, return to the grill for another minute or two.

Serve immediately, perhaps on a bed of rice cooked in chicken broth, or on a small plate garnished with a bouquet of fresh watercress. The tantalizing odors and textures, not to mention the tastes of this simple dish require a wine with the same elements. A young, fruity Beaujolais from France would be perfect, as would a California Gamay Beaujolais.

Yield: 16 to 20 skewers.

These can be broiled as well as grilled. Arrange about 3 inches below the broiling unit, and watch carefully to prevent burning.

CHICKEN LIVERS TERIYAKI

———— ❖❖❖ ————

This can be an hors d'oeuvre, arranged on small skewers, or a first course, arranged on larger skewers and served with rice.

1 *recipe teriyaki marinade (see page 50)*
2 *pounds fresh chicken livers, cleaned and quartered (see page 166)* (1 kilogram)

½ *pound bacon, cut into 1-inch-long pieces* (250 grams)

Prepare the teriyaki marinade, add the livers, and marinate overnight.

Preheat a grill to very hot.

Alternate the quartered livers with pieces of bacon on bamboo skewers, beginning and ending with a piece of bacon. Each skewer should hold 9 pieces of bacon and 8 pieces of liver. Dip the skewers in the marinade, and arrange on a grill, about 2 inches from the heat. Grill for 6 to 8 minutes, turning the livers once or twice so that they are evenly colored on all sides. Cut into a piece of liver in the middle of one of the skewers. It should be only slightly pink inside. If the liver still looks dark and raw, return it to the grill for another minute or two. Serve immediately on a bed of rice, or pass the skewers as an hors d'oeuvre.

As an hors d'oeuvre, serve with a well-chilled dry white wine such as California Chardonnay. As a main course, serve with a light, fruity red wine such as a California Gamay Beaujolais or an Italian Valpolicella.

Yield: about 16 to 20 skewers.

These can be broiled as well as grilled. Arrange about 3 inches below the broiling unit, and watch carefully to prevent burning.

KNISHES

———— ❖❖❖ ————

Lin Yutang said: "What is patriotism but the love of things we ate in our childhood." As a child I can remember being handed a hot—and for me at six years of age, enormous—knish, and bloating myself on it. I don't think I had eaten a knish for fifteen years until I began working on this recipe.

Knishes are a kind of Eastern European meat pie. These are filled with beef, liver, and buckwheat groats, and wrapped in a pastry made from mashed potatoes. They make excellent little hors d'oeuvres, and can be used as a garnish for meat or poultry, or soups.

THE PASTRY

1½ *pounds potatoes* (1 kilogram)
4 *Tablespoons rendered chicken fat or butter, melted*
2 *eggs*

2 *teaspoons salt*
1 *teaspoon freshly ground black pepper*
3 to 4 *cups all-purpose flour*

THE FILLING

4 *Tablespoons rendered chicken fat or oil*
1 *medium onion, finely chopped*
2 *garlic cloves, finely chopped*
½ *pound raw fresh chicken livers, cleaned and chopped (see page 166)* (250 grams)

½ *pound ground beef* (250 grams)
¾ *cup cooked buckwheat groats (kasha)*
Salt
Freshly ground black pepper

THE GLAZE

1 *egg beaten with* 1 *Tablespoon heavy cream*

Peel the potatoes and boil in water until tender. Drain, and transfer the potatoes to a large mixing bowl. Mash the potatoes as smooth as possible. Beat in the melted chicken fat or butter, then the eggs. Add the salt and pepper, and mix thoroughly. Add 2½ cups of the flour to the potatoes, and mix well. Gradually add enough additional flour, working it into the mixture with your hands, if necessary, to make a firm, but slightly sticky dough. Chill.

To prepare the filling, melt the chicken fat in a large skillet over medium to medium-high heat. Add the onions and garlic, and sauté, stirring occasionally, until the onions begin to brown on the edges. Add the liver and beef, and sauté, again stirring, for 2 to 3 minutes, until all of the red color of the raw beef has disappeared. Transfer to a large bowl. Stir in the buckwheat groats, and season with salt and pepper to taste.

Preheat oven to 400° F.

Place half the dough on a well-floured surface. Dust the top of the dough with additional flour, and roll it into a large rectangle, about ⅛ inch thick. With a pastry wheel or very sharp knife, cut the dough into strips, 2½ to 3 inches wide and 5 to 6 inches long.

Place a heaping tablespoon or so of the filling on half of each piece of dough, leaving a small border around the edge. Moisten the edges with a pastry brush dipped in water. Fold the top of the dough over the filling and press firmly into place. Trim the edges with a pastry wheel or very sharp knife. Arrange the knishes on a lightly greased baking sheet. Repeat with the remaining dough and filling.

When all of the knishes are made, brush the tops with the egg glaze. Bake in a preheated oven for 30 to 35 minutes.

Makes 25 to 30 knishes.

HEARTS AND GIZZARDS

———— ❖❖❖ ————

There are a great many uses for these two lovely morsels. They can be added to the stockpot, or used for any of the soup recipes from a simple broth or bouillon to a double consommé. They can be poached and added to stuffings and terrines. They can also be poached and crumbed in any of the breading mixtures in the section on fried chicken, pages 111–120, then fried in oil or fat until golden brown. Hearts and gizzards seem to be best when cooked by moist heat, although they can be roasted or grilled alongside the chicken and munched quietly by the cook in the kitchen. Hearts and gizzards can be used interchangeably in most recipes, though it does take a bit longer for the gizzards to cook. I often use them in salads, where they are not only unexpected, but colorful and delicious. Gizzards and hearts can also be poached, then marinated in the teriyaki marinade (see page 50), and either grilled or broiled on skewers as an hors d'oeuvre or first course. Sliced paper thin, they make an excellent addition to a Mongolian Hot Pot.

To Clean Hearts: Pick over the hearts, removing the sheer membrane and fat adhering to the outside. With a sharp knife, trim off the top of each heart. Rinse the hearts individually under cold running water, squeezing to eject any small clots of blood caught in the chambers. Pat dry.

To Clean Gizzards: Pick over the gizzards, removing the fat and discarding any that have been pierced during processing and still have grainy bits of the inner sack clinging to them. Although it is a tedious and time-consuming task, it is a good idea to remove the thick, yellowish sheathing. It can sometimes be peeled off, but usually needs to be trimmed with a very sharp knife. Rinse the gizzards under cold running water, cut in half, and pat dry.

HEART AND SAFFRON
RICE SALAD

❖❖❖

½ *pound hearts, cleaned as*
    directed (250 grams)
2 *cups chicken stock*
¼ *teaspoon saffron*
½ *teaspoon salt*
¼ *teaspoon freshly ground*
    black pepper
3 *Tablespoons oil*
1 *medium onion, finely*
    chopped

1 *cup rice*
3 *medium-sized tomatoes,*
    peeled, seeded, and coarsely
    chopped
½ *cup chopped green onions*
Vinaigrette dressing (see page
    213)

Add the cleaned hearts to boiling water, reduce the heat, and simmer until tender, about 1 hour. Drain, cool under cold running water, and pat dry. Chop the hearts with a large kitchen knife.

While the hearts are simmering, bring the stock to a boil with the saffron, salt, and pepper. Pour the oil into a saucepan and place over medium heat. When hot, add the onion and sauté until tender and translucent, about 2 minutes. Add the rice, and continue to sauté until most of the grains of rice appear opaque and bright white. Add the boiling saffron stock, stir together, cover tightly, and simmer until the rice has absorbed all of the liquid, about 20 minutes.

To assemble the salad, combine the saffron rice, tomato flesh, green onions, and hearts in a large bowl. Toss gently with a fork, not a spoon which will cause the grains of rice to stick together. Add the vinaigrette, and toss again.

Without the dressing, this salad makes an excellent side dish. With the dressing, serve cold. It's great for picnics.

RAGOUT OF GIZZARDS

———— ❖❖❖ ————

4 *Tablespoons oil*
1 *medium onion, finely*
  chopped
2 *Tablespoons flour*
2 *cups chicken stock*
½ *cup white wine*
Juice of half a small lemon
¼ *teaspoon crushed dried*
  thyme
2 *teaspoons mustard*
½ *teaspoon salt*

¼ *teaspoon freshly ground*
  black pepper
1 *pound gizzards, cleaned as*
  directed on page 177) (500
  grams)
3 *carrots, peeled and cut into*
  1-inch pieces
½ *pound potatoes, peeled and*
  cut into pieces about the
  size of the carrots (250
  grams)

Pour the oil into a large, preferably straight-sided skillet (with a cover) and place over medium heat. When the oil is hot, add the onions and sauté until tender and translucent, about 2 minutes. Stir in the flour, reduce the heat to low, and simmer for 2 to 3 minutes to remove the starchy taste of the raw flour, stirring occasionally. Add the stock, wine, lemon juice, thyme, mustard, salt, and pepper. Mix well, and bring to a boil, stirring occasionally so that the liquid thickens evenly and is free of lumps. When the liquid reaches a full boil, add the gizzards, reduce the heat, and simmer, partially covered, for 30 minutes. Add the carrots and potatoes, and simmer until tender, another 45 minutes to an hour.

Taste the sauce. Season with additional salt and pepper, and a little more lemon juice or mustard, if you wish. Serve hot with rice or buttered noodles. Serve with a lovely, rich, and full-bodied red wine from Burgundy, such as Morey-St.-Denis or Bonnes-Mares, or with a full-bodied Pinot Noir from California.

CHICKEN KIDNEYS

———— ❖❖❖ ————

Chicken "kidneys" are really testes. They have a smooth, delicate texture and taste. They are an acquired taste, and one which fewer and fewer people will ever be able to acquire. Because we breed chickens so rapidly today, the testicles do not grow large enough for cooking. But just in case you do happen upon some, here is a simple, delicious recipe which brings out their full flavor with a bit of cream and a little mustard, and complements the smooth, rich texture with the contrast of a buttery slice of fried bread. Serve this, if you dare, as a first course—but choose your dinner partners very carefully.

8 *Tablespoons butter*	1 *teaspoon Dijon mustard*
¼ *to* ½ *pound chicken testicles, split in half vertically (125–250 grams)*	*Salt*
	Freshly ground black pepper
¼ *cup heavy cream*	2 *slices white bread (crusts removed) fried in butter*

In a small saucepan, melt the butter over medium-low heat. Add the testicles, and cook until they become opaque in appearance and curl slightly around the edges as the thin outer membrane contracts, about 1–2 minutes. Shake the saucepan gently back and forth to prevent sticking.

Beat together the cream and mustard, and swirl into the saucepan. Season with salt and pepper, and cook only until the cream is hot. Spoon onto fried bread and serve immediately. Whomever you do serve this dish to deserves a beautiful wine to reward his or her courage. I'd recommend a white, dry, and elegant Chardonnay from California's Napa or Sonoma valleys.

Makes 2 servings.

CHICKEN CRACKLINGS

———— ❖❖❖ ————

Cracklings made from chicken skin can be used in the same way as pork cracklings are used, perhaps to garnish poached chicken. They can also be lightly salted and served with drinks in much the same way one would serve nuts or potato chips. They have a nice crispness, a light chicken flavor, and are not nearly so fatty as pork cracklings.

Chicken skin   *Salt*
Oil for deep frying

Spread the skin flat on a counter, and with a large, very sharp knife, cut into 1½-inch squares.

Pour enough oil into a large skillet to fill it to a depth of about 1 inch. Heat the oil to 375° F. Add the skin, a few pieces at a time, to the hot oil. Be careful of splattering. Fry the skin until crisp and a honey-brown color, about 4 minutes. Drain the skin on paper toweling, and sprinkle lightly with salt. Serve with beer or a jug of California Chablis, well chilled.

RENDERING CHICKEN FAT

———— ❖❖❖ ————

Rendered chicken fat can be used in much the same way butter or oil are used. It is good for sautéeing and browning, even for basting. Chickens need to be outdoors to develop large amounts of fat, and as most chickens available today have never seen the light of day or pecked at the ground for food, there is not much fat on them. But what bits of fat you do get can be frozen until you have accumulated enough to render them.

2 pounds chicken fat, diced   *2 medium onions, chopped*
   roughly into 1-inch pieces
   (1 kilogram)

In a large saucepan, combine the chicken fat with enough cold water to cover. Place over medium heat, cover the saucepan, and cook for 15 minutes. Uncover, raise the heat to medium-high, and boil until all the water has evaporated. Depending on the size of the pot and the amount of water added, this will take between 40 and 60 minutes. During the last 2 to 3 minutes of the boiling, the steam will begin to hiss as it is released from the fat, and the surface of the fat itself will roll and appear smooth and shiny yellow.

When all the water has evaporated, add the onion. Continue to boil over medium-high heat until the onion develops a golden-mahogany color, about 15 to 20 minutes. As soon as the onion has browned, remove the fat from the heat. When it has stopped boiling, carefully pour it through a strainer. Cool the fat to room temperature, then cover and refrigerate. The fat can be stored safely in the refrigerator for several months.

The onion and cracklings can also be saved. They make excellent additions to sauces and gravies, soups, chopped liver, and stuffings.

FEET AND COCKSCOMBS, KIDNEYS AND NECKS, AND UNBORN EGGS

❖❖❖

Federal legislation has prohibited the transportation of chicken feet across state lines unless they are specially processed, so they are not available for general sale. But it's not really any great loss. In the past, feet were used mainly for stock or soup, and occasionally thrown into a stew for extra body. Even with very long hours of simmering, they yield almost no flavor and less body and gelatin than one might suppose. Twelve chicken feet will yield roughly the same amount of gelatin and body as ½ pound of cracked veal knuckles. So that single pair of feet that was painstakingly scraped of scales and tossed into the stockpot really did almost nothing for the stock.

Cockscombs have also disappeared. Not only have they vir-

tually been eliminated from general sale by federal health restrictions, but cocks raised indoors mature so quickly that the
combs never grow large enough for cooking.

The necks make great stocks and soups. I have seen recipes for
poached, grilled, and broiled necks. The amount of meat on a
chicken neck is so small that I do not think they are good for
much except stocks and soups. The neck skins, if they haven't
been cut vertically in half during processing, can be stuffed and
used as sausage casings. But you'll need a lot of neck skins, as
the sausages will be tiny after the two ends are tied.

I have only found unborn eggs for sale once in my life, at
the Albert Cuypstraat Market in Amsterdam. These beautiful,
sweet little eggs are all yolk, with only a sheer outer membrane
holding them together. They are sweet-tasting with a rich texture and should be dropped whole into soups or stews. They'll
hard-cook in about 5 minutes.

8

SOUPS
AND STOCKS

———————— ❖❖❖ ————————

Soups have been the stalwart of American cooking for the last two centuries. There were early game soups and vegetable soups, and later cream soups; there were fish soups and the famous chowders of New England and the gumbos of the Deep South.

There's a good deal of confusion about the differences between a stock, a broth, a bouillon, a consommé, and a double consommé. A stock is the weakest of the lot. It is simply water which has been given some body and flavor by simmering it with bones and vegetables. A stock is far too bland to be eaten as a soup, and is used as a base for something else—a liquid for poaching or stewing, or for soups. Stock is left underseasoned. The recipe in this chapter, though it may look skimpy on the ingredients list, produces an extraordinarily full-flavored stock.

A broth is next on the list, if we consider them in sequence of strength, from weakest to strongest. It has a stronger, rounder, more balanced flavor than stock. It is thin, relatively clear, and fully seasoned. One of the simplest ways to make a broth is to reduce some stock by half. Another way, which I prefer, is to enrich the stock by simmering it again with fresh bones and vegetables. The recipe for Jewish chicken soup is a good example of a broth. Broth and bouillon are exactly the same.

A consommé is stronger than a broth. You can reduce a broth to make a consommé, but again, I prefer to reinforce it with more bones. A consommé must be absolutely clear, shimmering and golden. To obtain this visual purity, it is clarified with egg white, a simple process which is explained in full in the recipe for consommé.

A jellied consommé is simply a consommé which has been slightly overseasoned and chilled until its natural gelatin sets.

A double consommé is the boldest and richest soup in this sequence. It has all the qualities of a consommé—strength, purity, and clarity—but it has a stronger flavor, and its natural gelatin should cling to your mouth as you swallow.

There are recipes for all of these, in addition to some other chicken soups. There are thousands of soups which use chicken stock or broth as a base, but I have limited the recipes here to a few soups which call for both chicken stock or broth, and chicken in the soup.

RICH CHICKEN STOCK

———— ❖❖❖ ————

Most recipes for stock have long lists of ingredients—bones of various descriptions, including a cracked veal knuckle; a veritable grocery of aromatic vegetables, including onions, carrots, celery, leeks, turnips, parsnips; then there's the parsley and the garlic, the bay leaf and the thyme, the cloves, and the salt and pepper. But out of that whole list you need only four ingredients to make a beautiful, rich, homemade stock, and I sometimes wonder if two of those ingredients are even necessary.

The carcass of one 2½-pound   *Salt*
   chicken (1 kilogram)   *Freshly ground black pepper*
2 quarts cold water (2 liters)

Break the carcass into a few pieces so it fits easily into a pot. Add the cold water and place on a thermostatically controlled burner set at its lowest setting. After 12 to 15 hours, strain the stock and taste it. It might need a little salt and will probably need a few grinds of pepper. Stock should be underseasoned. It is a base, rather than an end in itself, and will be fully seasoned when it is used in a recipe. Refrigerate or freeze until needed. Stock should not be stored in the refrigerator for more than 3 to 4 days.

Yield: 1½ quarts rich, homemade stock.

If you are serious about making stock, you will usually have more than just a small carcass on hand. Use all the bones, backs, necks, gizzards, and feet you want. Three pounds of bones should yield about a gallon of stock.

A WORD OF CAUTION: The first time you try this recipe, check the stock every couple of hours to see that your burner does not cause the water to evaporate before the stock has finished cooking, and that the liquid is just below the boil. Also, do not use bones with large amounts of flesh on them unless they are cooked first—raw chicken simmered this way will sour. At the slightest sign of souring, discard the stock.

TWO ALTERNATIVE WAYS TO MAKE STOCK

METHOD ONE

Stock is something you should learn to make casually from saved bones and other bits and pieces, and whatever vegetables are on hand. Never feel bound to an ingredients list.

Place about 3 pounds of bones, necks, gizzards, etc. (not livers) in a large pot with a few ribs of celery, a couple of carrots, and a large onion. Add 4 to 5 quarts of cold water and bring slowly to a boil over medium heat, uncovered. When the liquid reaches a full boil, reduce the heat to low, and simmer, partially covered, for 4 to 5 hours. Strain, and underseason by adding just a little salt and freshly ground black pepper.

Makes about a gallon.

METHOD TWO

The recipe for Jewish chicken soup on page 191 can easily be turned into a beautiful stock by combining all the ingredients in a 10- to 12-quart pot and filling with cold water. Cooked as directed in the recipe, it'll make about 8 quarts of stock.

CHICKEN GLAZE
OR PORTABLE CHICKEN SOUP

❖❖❖

A chicken glaze is simply stock reduced to about an eighth or tenth of its original volume. As it reduces, it becomes a dark, gooey syrup, and when chilled it becomes very much like a chunk of hard rubber. But what a chunk-o'-rubber!

It's a great space-saver, and perfect to have on hand. My friends call it "homemade bouillon *cubes*": the nineteenth-century American cookbook author, Miss Leslie, would have called it Portable Chicken Soup, and the French think of it as *glace de poulet*.

A walnut-size chunk of the glaze mixed with a cup of hot water is instant chicken soup; mixed with a pint of water, it's instant stock. Rice or pasta can be cooked in water and then tossed with a piece of the glaze for more chicken flavor than if it had been boiled in stock. It can be used to enrich and flavor sauces, gravies, and pan drippings. It can be added to fricassees, stews, and chicken pies. Extra stuffing that won't fit into the chicken can be baked in the oven and then tossed with some glaze. It can even be heated and painted onto a cold chicken in place of a *chaud-froid* sauce.

The glaze can be refrigerated in a tightly covered jar for up to 2 months, and can be safely kept in the freezer for 3 to 4 months.

1 *gallon rich, homemade*
   chicken stock (4 liters)

Chill a gallon of rich, homemade stock overnight. Carefully remove all of the fat that congeals on the top. Pour the stock into a large pot and place over medium-high heat, stirring occasionally until the stock liquifies. Allow the stock to boil slowly until it is reduced to about 1 quart, about 2 to 2½ hours.

Strain into a small saucepan through a sieve lined with cheese-cloth. Place back over medium heat, and reduce to 1½ to 2 cups, skimming occasionally. The glaze will become thick, dark, and syrupy. Cool to room temperature, then refrigerate until needed.

JEWISH CHICKEN SOUP
(*for a large amount of broth or bouillon*)

———————— ❖❖❖ ————————

This is what is often referred to as Jewish penicillin, though you don't have to be sick to enjoy a bowl of this beautiful broth.

1 *fowl, cut in* 8 *to* 10 *pieces*	2 *bay leaves, crumbled*
3 *celery ribs*	1 *Tablespoon crushed dried*
3 *carrots*	*thyme*
2 *medium onions, root end*	1 *Tablespoon salt*
trimmed and cut in half	1 *teaspoon freshly ground*
5 *to* 6 *parsley sprigs*	*black pepper*
2 *garlic cloves, unpeeled*	*Cold water*

Combine all ingredients in a large pot, about 8 quarts. Fill with cold water, and place over medium heat. When the water comes to a boil, reduce the heat and simmer, partially covered, for 4 to 5 hours. Pour the soup through a strainer lined with cheesecloth or a kitchen towel. Taste the soup. If you want a stronger soup, place it over medium-high heat and reduce it by a quarter to a third. Season with additional salt and pepper to taste. Chill, and remove the congealed fat on top of the soup. This soup can be safely refrigerated for several days, or frozen and kept for 3 to 4 months.

Makes about 4 quarts.

Soups are frequently served without wine, but a very traditional and exciting accompaniment to most clear soups is a fine, extremely dry Fino Sherry from Spain. Or, if this is to be served in an Orthodox Jewish home, a dry Sherry from Israel would be fine, and, of course, it would be kosher.

For additional flavor, add 3 to 4 cups of dry white wine to the water. Another favorite way of flavoring the soup is to add

2 ounces of Cognac to each quart of soup, and then to simmer it for 5 minutes before serving.

VARIATIONS

CHICKEN NOODLE SOUP: For each quart of chicken soup, add 1 to 2 cups of cooked noodles or soup pasta, and ¾ cup finely diced cooked chicken.

CHICKEN VEGETABLE SOUP: For a richer, more filling soup, excellent for a light supper or lunch on a cold day, any number of vegetables can be cooked in the soup just before serving. Some of my favorites are chopped spinach leaves, finely shredded cabbage or Chinese cabbage, mushrooms and peas, in addition to the cooked noodles or rice and diced chicken.

CREAM OF CHICKEN SOUP: Place a quart of chicken soup over medium-high heat and reduce by a quarter to a third. Stir in 1 cup heavy cream. Place 3 egg yolks in a mixing bowl. Gradually beat a cup of the soup into the egg yolks. Reverse the process, gradually beating the egg yolks into the soup. Add 2 cups finely diced cooked chicken. Place over medium-low heat. Stirring the whole time, heat the soup until it thickens and you see the first vapors of steam rising from the surface. Do not let the soup come to a boil or the eggs will scramble. Remove from the heat, taste, and season with salt and pepper. Serve immediately.

CONSOMMÉ

———————— ❖❖❖ ————————

There are two ways to make a consommé. One is to reduce a simple broth, such as the one produced in the recipe for Jewish chicken soup, by about half. This will concentrate the flavor to that of a consommé, which would then need clarifying. The second technique, which I prefer, is to enrich a broth by simmering it with additional bones, and then clarify it.

TO MAKE A CONSOMMÉ BY SIMMERING: Place 2 to 3 pounds of miscellaneous chicken bones and giblets (not the liver) in a large pot. Cover with 4 to 5 quarts cold chicken broth or rich homemade stock, bring slowly to a boil, reduce heat, and simmer, partially covered, for 4 to 5 hours. Season with salt and pepper to taste, then clarify as directed below.

To CLARIFY A CONSOMMÉ: You'll need 2 egg whites plus their shells (crushed) *for each quart of consommé.*

Pour the consommé into a large pot, and bring to a boil over medium-high heat. Remove from the heat while you beat the egg whites.

Place the egg whites and their crushed shells in a large bowl and beat with a wire whisk until frothy and almost doubled in bulk, about 1 minute. Pour the egg whites into the consommé, and place back over medium-high heat. Beat and stir the consommé until it comes to a rolling boil and the egg whites rise in a high froth. Immediately remove from the heat and allow to rest, undisturbed, for 5 to 10 minutes. This gives the soup a chance to separate from the shells and egg whites, to which all of the impurities are now clinging.

Gently ladle the soup and eggs into a sieve lined with cheesecloth or a kitchen towel. The crisp, clean, shimmering golden liquid will drip through the cheesecloth very slowly, so be patient. Reheat, and serve immediately, or store in the refrigerator or freezer until needed.

There is nothing quite as superlative as Sherry with soup. In fact, this is such an excellent amalgam of flavors that many people prefer to pour most of their Sherry into the soup itself. There is no doubt that an ounce or two enhances all the soup's flavors.

DOUBLE CONSOMMÉ

The recipe for the above consommé is very rich, and by many standards approaches a double consommé in texture and flavor. But should you want a double consommé for a very special dinner, simply reduce the soup used for making the consommé above by half, and then clarify. Serve very hot, and in small quantities, as it will be far too rich to eat much of. It should be accompanied by a fine Fino Sherry.

JELLIED CONSOMMÉ OR CHICKEN JELLY

❖❖❖

This is a beautiful and elegant first course for a luncheon on a warm day. It is actually nothing more than a slightly overseasoned consommé, chilled until jellied, and served on a bed of lettuce.

> 1 *recipe Chicken Consommé*
> *Lettuce and watercress for*
> *garnish*

Prepare one recipe of consommé, but overseason slightly with salt and pepper. Refrigerate the consommé until it sets. With a large, sharp knife, finely chop the jelly. Mound the chicken jelly on a bed of lettuce and garnish with a few sprigs of crisp, fresh watercress.

I'd drink a fine Fino Sherry with this dish, but an extremely dry, very crisp, not very flowery white wine such as a Muscadet would also be good.

CHICKEN DUMPLING SOUP

❖❖❖

These lovely, light, delicately flavored chicken dumplings are simple to make and can be made a day or two ahead and simply reheated in the soup a few minutes before serving.

> 8 *ounces raw chicken, prefer-*
> *ably white meat, finely*
> *chopped or ground (250*
> *grams)*
> 2 *cups fresh white bread*
> *crumbs, made from bread*
> *with crusts removed*

> 4 *Tablespoons melted butter*
> 2 *teaspoons salt*
> ½ *teaspoon freshly ground*
> *black pepper*
> *Dash of nutmeg*
> 2 *eggs, well beaten*
> *Flour*

Combine the chicken, bread crumbs, butter, salt, pepper and a dash of nutmeg in a large bowl. Stir in the eggs, and mix well. With lightly floured hands, shape the dumplings into balls about the size of a walnut.

Add the dumplings to lightly salted boiling water. Reduce the heat, and simmer for 25 to 30 minutes. Remove the dumplings with a slotted spoon, and drain on paper toweling. Either add to hot chicken soup and serve immediately, or cover and refrigerate until needed. A dry Fino Sherry would be a lovely accompaniment.

Yield: about 20 small dumplings.

COCK-A-LEEKIE

❖❖❖

This was a traditional Scottish solution to the problem of what to do with the old barnyard cock—alleged to be tougher than an old hen. The cock was placed in a pot with a small chunk of stewing beef, covered with sliced leeks, and the whole covered in water and simmered for 5 hours. A few prunes were added during the last hour of the cooking for sweetening and flavoring.

This is a big soup, rich with the flavor of the fowl and the beef, and filled with cooked meat. Serve it as a meal in itself, with fresh, homemade bread and sweet butter.

1 *fowl, cut into serving pieces,*   *Salt*
   excess fat removed (see   *Freshly ground black pepper*
   page 224)   *½ pound, exactly, pitted*
2 *pounds shin of beef, cut in*   *prunes (250 grams)*
   5 or 6 pieces (1 kilogram)
18 *to* 24 *small- to medium-*
   sized leeks, dark-green tops
   removed, cleaned, and
   thinly sliced

Combine the fowl, beef, leeks, 2 tablespoons of salt and 2 teaspoons pepper in a very large pot, about 12 quarts. Cover with cold water.

Bring to a boil over medium-high heat. Reduce heat, and simmer, partially covered, for 4 hours.

With a slotted spoon or tongs, remove the beef and chicken. Add the prunes, and simmer 45 minutes. While the prunes are simmering, allow the beef and chicken to cool. When cool enough to handle, in about 30 minutes, pick over the chicken and beef, remove the bones, skin, and any gristle in the beef, and shred or dice the meats. Return the meats to the soup, and season to taste. The soup will probably need a lot of salt and pepper. Skim as much of the fat off the top as possible, and simmer 15 minutes longer.

Heaven knows what the Scots serve with their Cock-a-Leekie, but my recommendation would be a robust red wine such as a Riserva Chianti *classico* from Italy to stand up to all those heady flavors.

Makes about 7 quarts.

CHICKEN MINESTRONE

———— ❖❖❖ ————

Minestrone is by tradition a vegetable soup—thick and filling and a meal in itself. This is a delicious variation on it, using chicken stock as the base and adding finely diced chicken. Whenever I think of minestrone I am reminded of a party I attended in San Francisco in 1975. It was a sit-down dinner for 65 people, with a creative and ingenious hostess whose invitation listed the menu: Minestrone with Grated Parmesan, Cheese and Fresh Fruit, Chocolate Cake and Coffee. It was a simple, but delicious dinner, and a perfect solution to the problem of single-handedly preparing dinner for a large group. I'm sure the hostess, Marion Cunningham, would not in the least mind you copying her idea.

¼ cup oil

1 large onion, chopped

3 garlic cloves, finely chopped

2 celery ribs, diced

3 carrots, diced

2 zucchini, split and thinly sliced

2 large potatoes (about ¾ pound), peeled and diced

2 leeks, cleaned and thinly sliced

4 ounces ham, diced (125 grams)

2 quarts chicken stock (2 liters)

1 can (about 12 to 14 ounces) peeled, Italian tomatoes, drained (about 350 grams)

1 Tablespoon crushed dried basil

2 teaspoons salt

½ teaspoon freshly ground black pepper

1 cup cooked Great Northern beans

½ cup elbow macaroni, or small soup pasta

3 cups chicken, finely diced (either raw or cooked)

Grated Parmesan cheese for garnish

Pour the oil into a large pot over medium heat. Add the onion and garlic, and sauté until golden and just beginning to brown along the edges, about 6 minutes. Add the celery, carrots, zucchini, potatoes, leeks, and ham, and sauté for 5 to 6 minutes. Add the stock, tomatoes, basil, salt, and pepper. Bring the soup to a boil, then reduce the heat, and simmer for 2½ to 3 hours. Add the beans, macaroni, and chicken, and simmer until the macaroni is tender, about 10 minutes. Taste the soup, and add more salt and pepper as needed. Serve hot, accompanied by a bowl of freshly grated Parmesan cheese.

The soup can be stored in the refrigerator for several days, or frozen in small containers, if you wish. In Italy—and minestrone is Italian—this soup is frequently cooked with a full-bodied, robust, even harsh red wine, which is also used to accompany the soup. The French, on the other hand, often don't serve soup with wine, but I like wine with my soup, especially a chewy one such as minestrone. A Chianti from Tuscany, in Italy, would be nice, or even a jug Chianti from California.

GIBLET SOUP

———— ❖❖❖ ————

Just a hint of mustard in this soup makes all the difference.

1 *pound giblets (not livers)* (500 grams)
1 *quart chicken stock* (1 liter)
3 *Tablespoons butter or oil*
½ *medium onion, finely chopped*
1 *small celery rib, finely chopped*
½ *small green pepper, finely chopped*
1 *garlic clove, finely chopped*
2 *Tablespoons flour*
1 *teaspoon mustard*
Salt
Freshly ground black pepper

Clean the giblets, removing any excess fat or blood. Add the giblets to the stock, and bring to a boil over medium-high heat. Reduce the heat, and simmer for 1 hour, skimming occasionally.

While the giblets are cooking, melt the butter or oil in a saucepan. When hot, add the onion, celery, green pepper, and garlic, and sauté over medium-low heat until tender and translucent, about 6 minutes. Reduce heat to low, and stir in the flour. Cook for 2 minutes, stirring the whole time. Allow the vegetables to cool in the saucepan while the giblets finish cooking.

Place the saucepan with the cooked vegetables over medium-high heat. Strain the stock into the vegetables, and stir until the soup comes to a boil. Reduce heat to low, and simmer.

Clean the cooked giblets, removing the gristle and fat. Dice the giblets, and add to the soup. Stir in the mustard; taste, and add salt and pepper as needed. Simmer 1 minute longer. Serve hot.

I'd serve this unusual soup with either an Amontillado Sherry, which is round and full without being sweet (in fact, you might want to pour two thimblefuls into the soup, it's delicious), or with a dry white Mâcon Blanc from France.

Makes about 1 quart.

9

SAUCES

——— ❖❖❖ ———

THERE ARE FIVE important families of sauces for home cooking: the white sauces, the egg-emulsion sauces—hollandaise- and
mayonnaise-based sauces—the vinaigrette or oil-and-vinegar-
based sauces, the tomato sauces, and the brown sauces. Once
you've learned to make the basic, or mother, sauce in each family, the rest of the sauces in that group require only minor
changes in flavorings and seasonings. When chicken is accompanied by a sauce, it usually will be a white sauce or an egg-
emulsion sauce.

To avoid lumpy sauces, simply remember that the roux and
the liquid should have opposite temperatures. If the liquid is hot,
stir it into a roux that has been cooled. If the liquid is cold, add
it to a hot roux that has just finished simmering.

WHITE SAUCES

——— ❖❖❖ ———

In French cooking, the basic white sauce is called the *sauce
velouté*. The word *velouté* means "made soft and velvet-like in
texture." This velvety texture comes from thickening the sauce
with a roux. A roux is simply melted butter and flour stirred
together to form a paste, and then simmered to remove the
starchy taste of raw flour. When liquid is added to a roux and
they are heated together, a chemical reaction takes place. Each
of the tiny starch particles of the flour absorbs hundreds of
times its weight in liquid, resulting in thousands of liquid-filled
beads which cling together. This is what thickens the sauce and
gives it the rich velvetlike texture.

BASIC WHITE SAUCE

❖❖❖

MASTER RECIPE

❖

This is one of the most frequently used sauces in chicken recipes.

3 *Tablespoons butter*   *Salt*
3 *Tablespoons flour*   *Freshly ground black pepper*
2 *cups cold chicken stock*

Melt the butter in a saucepan over medium-low heat. When hot, add the flour, and stir to form a smooth paste. Reduce the heat slightly, and simmer the roux for 4 to 5 minutes, stirring occasionally, to remove the raw, starchy taste of the flour.

When the roux has finished simmering, it should be a golden-yellow color. Stir in the stock. As a general rule, add cold liquid to a hot roux, and hot liquid to a cold roux to prevent lumping. Slowly bring the sauce to a boil, stirring to prevent scorching. Once it comes to a complete boil, it is fully thickened. Season with salt and pepper to taste. Cook for 1 minute longer, and taste again to make certain the seasoning is correct.

That is all there is to making a basic white sauce, but you can refine and improve it for special occasions in the following ways:

SIMMERING: One method is to simmer the sauce very slowly. A really great sauce may have simmered for 4 to 5 hours, but even 15 to 30 minutes of simmering will noticeably improve the texture. During the simmering, the sauce should be skimmed frequently, and just before serving it should be beaten with a whisk and poured through a fine strainer.

TO ENRICH A SAUCE WITH BUTTER: Another way to improve the character of a sauce is to enrich it with butter. Just before serving, lift the sauce from the heat and swirl in 2 tablespoons of butter, cut in bits, for each cup of sauce. Swirl the butter gently in the sauce until completely melted and mixed with the sauce. This gives the sauce a richer flavor and a shimmering softness. The butter enrichment should always be the last step in making a sauce. It can be done whether or not the sauce has been simmered.

To ENRICH A SAUCE WITH EGG YOLKS: The addition of egg yolks to a sauce not only enriches the flavor of the sauce but thickens it further. Any white sauce can be enriched in this way.

Prepare the sauce as directed in the recipe. When the sauce has reached the boiling point, remove it from the heat. Beat 3 egg yolks in a bowl, and gradually beat about a cup of the sauce into the yolks. Do this slowly so that the temperature of the yolks is gradually and evenly raised. Now reverse the process, and pour the egg mixture back into the remaining sauce, stirring constantly. Place the sauce over medium heat, and bring back to a boil, stirring the whole time and scraping the bottom of the saucepan to prevent sticking. When the sauce comes to a boil, taste and adjust the seasonings.

REDUCING THE STOCK: To give the sauce a richer taste, the stock is often reduced to half its original volume. For additional flavor add some fresh or dried herbs to the stock before reducing it, then strain and proceed with the recipe. Broth or consommé can be used instead of stock.

The master recipe is for a medium-thick sauce. If you prefer a thinner sauce, use only 2 tablespoons of butter and 2 of flour. For a thicker sauce use 4 tablespoons of butter and 4 of flour. If the sauce is to be used for a chicken sauté, or any other preparation where additional liquid is to be added, then a slightly thicker sauce should be made.

WHITE SAUCE WITH
MILK AND STOCK

❖❖❖

Good with poached or roast chicken, this is a simple variation on the basic white sauce.

Prepare the basic white sauce as directed in the master recipe (see page 202), using 1 cup of milk and 1 cup of stock for the liquid.

This sauce can be simmered, or enriched with butter or egg yolks, if you wish.

CREAM SAUCE

―――――― ❖❖❖ ――――――

Prepare the basic white sauce as directed in the master recipe (see page 202), using 1 cup of milk and 1 cup of cream, or 2 cups of cream for the liquid. The proportion of milk to cream will depend on how rich you want the sauce.

This sauce can be simmered, or enriched with butter or egg yolks, if you wish.

MUSTARD SAUCE

―――――― ❖❖❖ ――――――

Mustard: Good only in Dijon.
Ruins the Stomach.
FLAUBERT

This is a lovely sauce for roast, poached, or broiled chicken. But the quality of the mustard is important, so use a good mustard from Dijon or a Meaux.

Prepare a white sauce or cream sauce as directed in the recipes above. When the sauce has come to a boil and is fully thickened, stir in 2 to 3 tablespoons of mustard. The sauce should have a distinct mustard flavor, but should not be overwhelmingly mustardy. Taste the sauce, then season with salt and pepper.

PARSLEY SAUCE

———— ❖❖❖ ————

Good with poached or roasted chicken, a parsley sauce is most easily made with a white sauce or cream sauce as the base, but it can also be prepared from a lightly flavored mustard sauce.

Prepare a white sauce or cream sauce as directed in the recipes above. When the sauce comes to the boil and is fully thickened, stir in ½ cup chopped parsley and ¼ cup chopped fresh chives. Season with salt and pepper to taste.

VARIATIONS

DILL SAUCE: Substitute chopped fresh dill for the parsley in the above recipe.

TARRAGON SAUCE: Substitute tarragon for the parsley in the above recipe.

I think the tarragon sauce is best made with a cream-sauce base and enriched with butter.

Any of these sauces would also go well with poached or baked fish—striped bass, sole, halibut, and the like.

MAYONNAISE AND HOLLANDAISE SAUCES

———— ❖❖❖ ————

Mayonnaise and hollandaise are the two main egg-emulsion sauces—that is, sauces that use eggs rather than flour or starch for thickening.

This is what happens when you make a mayonnaise or hollandaise. Under a microscope, an egg-emulsion sauce looks like thousands and thousands of tiny balloons touching each other. The balloons are made of egg and filled with oil or fat. When you beat the first few drops of oil or butter into the egg yolks, the egg moves around the oil and seals it in a balloon. If you add too much oil, or add it too quickly, the balloons pop. And that first pop causes a chain reaction that pops all the other balloons, causing the sauce to curdle. If you keep that image in mind when you make the sauce—and remember not to add too much oil, or too quickly, and to beat well after each addition—there won't be any problem.

The mayonnaise recipe calls for eggs and oil at room temperature. This makes it easier for the sauce to emulsify. In the hollandaise sauce, hot butter is added to warmed egg yolks, and as long as you don't accidentally scramble the eggs by overheating them, you will have no trouble with the emulsification.

With either of these sauces, the faster the sauce is beaten, the smaller and smaller the balloons become, and the more of those tiny touching beads there are. For this reason, a mayonnaise made with a fork will have the largest beads, and will have a rich, velvety texture, but can never really be smooth. Making the sauce with a wire whisk will produce a much smoother texture, but obviously not nearly so smooth as one made in a blender or food processor. Basically the same holds true of hollandaise. So whether you prepare these sauces by hand, or in a blender or food processor, is simply a matter of which final texture you want—and to a lesser degree which final flavor you prefer, as sauces made by hand usually have a slightly greater egg taste.

The yolk of a large egg can hold about a cup of oil or fat. The recipes in this book are deliberately designed to stay safely below that. But should the sauce break, beat a fresh egg yolk in a clean bowl for a few seconds to thicken it. Then gradually beat in the oil and egg yolk of the broken sauce. The sauce will re-emulsify.

Why not make some mayonnaise right now? There is no one watching, and no pressure on you, and you will feel great for having conquered your first emulsion sauce. You can store it in the refrigerator for a few days until you find a use for it, so it won't go to waste.

MAYONNAISE

— ❖❖❖ —

Mayonnaise serves the French in
place of a state religion.

This fantastic sauce made its debut in the mid-eighteenth century and is one of the most versatile and exciting creations of the saucier's repertoire. Use with cold chicken, for making salads, or as otherwise directed in a recipe.

HANDMADE MAYONNAISE

— ❖❖❖ —

MASTER RECIPE

— ❖ —

3 egg yolks, at room temperature
1 Tablespoon lemon juice or vinegar

Salt
Freshly ground black pepper
1½ to 2 cups oil, at room temperature

Place the yolks in a bowl and beat with a wire whisk or an electric beater for a minute or so until they thicken to about the consistency of heavy cream. Add the lemon juice, ½ teaspoon of salt, and some pepper, and beat 30 seconds longer. (A damp towel placed under the bowl will help keep it from jumping around as you beat in the oil.)

Begin dribbling the oil into the yolks, a few drops at a time, beating well after each addition until the oil binds with the yolks. Continue adding the oil, a few drops at a time, and beating well after each addition until the mayonnaise begins to thicken and about ½ a cup of the oil has been incorporated. You can now safely relax and give your wrist a rest.

Gradually add the rest of the oil, increasing the amount added each time, but never adding more than a teaspoon or two at once. Beat well after each addition. When all of the oil has been incorporated, taste the sauce and adjust the seasonings. You may want to add a little more lemon juice or vinegar, or simply adjust the amount of salt and peppr. Should the sauce have become too thick, thin it with a little hot water or more lemon juice.

Yield: about 2 cups.

LEMON-FLAVORED MAYONNAISE

This is a lovely variation on the basic mayonnaise, with a refreshing tartness and a crisp, clean flavor.

Flavor 2 cups of mayonnaise, prepared by hand as directed in the master recipe, see above, or made in a blender or food processor, by beating in 2 to 3 tablespoons of freshly squeezed lemon juice.

Taste the sauce: it should be distinctly lemony in flavor, but not so tart that it makes one's mouth pucker.

MUSTARD-FLAVORED MAYONNAISE

This is one of my favorite mayonnaise variations. It is not only great with chicken, but perfect for all kinds of salads, sandwiches, and fish.

Flavor 2 cups of mayonnaise by beating in 2 to 4 tablespoons of mustard. The amount of mustard added will depend on the type and strength of the mustard, and the richness of the mayonnaise, so taste as you add.

GARLIC MAYONNAISE

———— ❖❖❖ ————

This is known in French as sauce *aïoli*. Traditionally the *aïoli* is made by pounding the garlic and egg yolks in a mortar, and then pestling in the oil. But there are other alternatives.

Depending on your love for garlic, use 2 to 4 garlic cloves for 2 cups of mayonnaise. The simplest method is to chop the garlic very, very finely, or to pound it into a paste with a few drops of oil, and stir it into the mayonnaise. In this case, the mayonnaise should be allowed to mellow overnight. The garlic can also be swirled in a blender with 3 to 4 tablespoons of oil, and then beaten into a finished mayonnaise. In this case, prepare the mayonnaise with a little less oil than usual. The easiest way to make a garlic mayonnaise is in the food processor. Simply put the garlic and the eggs in the food processor, and then prepare the mayonnaise.

HERB MAYONNAISE

———— ❖❖❖ ————

A great way to add variation to the flavor of a basic mayonnaise is to stir in finely chopped fresh herbs.

To 2 cups of mayonnaise add ¼ to ½ cup finely chopped fresh tarragon, chives, basil, parsley, dill, or any other fresh herb you wish. Various herbs in combination with each other are also good—perhaps some tarragon and chives, with a hint of garlic, or a parsley mayonnaise with a little rosemary for flavor and fragrance.

This is a great place to use whatever fresh herbs are available and to create your own new flavors each time.

MAYONNAISE WITH CAPERS, GARLIC, AND ONION

———— ❖❖❖ ————

This is a full-flavored mayonnaise. It is good with cold chicken, particularly with chicken salads.

To 2 cups of mayonnaise, either prepared by hand as directed in the master recipe, page 207, or made in a blender or food processor, add 2 tablespoons finely chopped capers, 2 tablespoons finely chopped parsley, 1 garlic clove, finely chopped, 2 tablespoons finely chopped shallots or ⅓ cup finely chopped chives, and 2 tablespoons finely chopped gherkins. Allow the sauce to mellow for an hour or so before serving.

SAUCE RÉMOULADE: To make a rémoulade sauce, add a teaspoon or two of finely chopped and mashed canned anchovy fillets to the mayonnaise above.

HOLLANDAISE SAUCE

———— ❖❖❖ ————

Many people shy away from the thought of making a hollandaise. They have read it is a "finicky" sauce, a "tricky" sauce, a "temperamental emulsion." Perhaps it is a bit of all of these. But if you don't think about what might go wrong with your hollandaise, it won't.

HANDMADE HOLLANDAISE

———— ❖❖❖ ————

16 *Tablespoons butter*   ¼ *teaspoon salt*
3 *egg yolks*   *Freshly ground black pepper*
1 *Tablespoon lemon juice*

Melt the butter in a small saucepan over medium-low heat. As soon as the butter is fully melted and begins to boil, remove from the heat.

In a heavy-bottomed saucepan, combine the yolks, lemon juice, salt, and a few grinds of pepper. Place the saucepan over low heat, and beat with a wire whisk until the yolks thicken and feel warm, not hot, to the touch. (If you stick your finger into the egg yolks at this point, they will feel warm or perhaps just a little bit more than warm, but certainly not hot. That is as high as the temperature of the sauce should ever be—and for hollandaise, your finger must be your thermometer.)

Lift the saucepan off the heat. Dribble a few drops of the hot butter into the yolks, whisking hard until it binds into the egg yolks. Gradually increase the amount of butter added until you are adding about a teaspoon at a time. Whisk well after each addition. It will begin to bind and thicken after about 3 tablespoons of the butter have been added.

When you have added about ¼ cup of the butter, place the sauce over low heat and whisk hard until the sauce warms up again. This should take about 15 or 20 seconds. As soon as the sauce feels warm, lift it off the heat and begin adding more butter. Each time ¼ cup of butter has been added, rewarm the sauce. When all of the butter has been incorporated, taste the sauce. It may need a little more lemon juice.

Yield: about 1½ cups, enough for 4 to 6 people.

MUSTARD HOLLANDAISE

❖❖❖

The addition of mustard is a welcome variation on the basic hollandaise. It goes particularly well with roast or poached chicken or with poached fish.

Prepare the hollandaise sauce as directed in the master recipe, page 211. When all of the butter has been added, flavor the sauce with 1 to 2 tablespoons of mustard.

MOUSSELINE SAUCE

❖❖❖

Whipped cream folded into a hollandaise just before serving changes it into a mousseline sauce. It is a lighter, more delicate sauce that goes well with mousses, mousselines, quenelles, many kinds of fish, and poached chicken.

Prepare the hollandaise as directed in the master recipe, page 211. Just before serving, fold ½ cup of whipped cream into the sauce. Serve immediately.

HOT OR COLD DEVILED HOLLANDAISE SAUCE

❖❖❖

This sauce is excellent rushed to the table just as the last few drops of butter are incorporated. But it is also beautiful later, served at room temperature. Hot, serve it with poached chicken; cold, with cold poached or roasted chicken, or hot broiled or grilled chicken.

Prepare the hollandaise sauce as directed in the master recipe, page 211. Just before serving, stir in ½ teaspoon of mustard and a heaping tablespoon each of gherkins, capers, and onion or shallot, all very finely chopped.

BÉARNAISE SAUCE

❖❖❖

Béarnaise is a hollandaise flavored with a reduction of shallots, tarragon, white wine, and vinegar. The traditional accompaniment for grilled meat and fish, it is also excellent with grilled or broiled chicken.

In a heavy saucepan, combine ½ cup of white wine, ¼ cup vinegar, 2 tablespoons finely chopped shallots, and 1 tablespoon of crushed dried tarragon or ¼ cup finely chopped fresh tarragon. Place the saucepan over medium heat and reduce the liquid to about 2 tablespoons. Strain and return the liquid to the saucepan. Remove the saucepan from the heat and allow it to cool for 5 minutes. Now add the egg yolks, a little salt and pepper, and proceed to make a hollandaise as directed in the master recipe (see page 211).

MINT-FLAVORED BEARNAISE: This is an interesting variation that I am particularly fond of in the spring and summer months. Substitute mint for the tarragon in the reduction.

VINAIGRETTE SAUCES

❖❖❖

Vinaigrettes are uncooked sauces, simple mixtures of oil and vinegar, or oil and lemon juice. Everyone has his own idea of how much tang a vinaigrette should have. I remember a New York food writer once saying she liked 1 part vinegar to 2 parts oil. For me that's overwhelmingly acidic, and I prefer 1 part vinegar to 8 parts oil. But the acid level, whether you are using vinegar or lemon juice, is a strictly personal matter, and the choice is yours. Whatever ratio you choose—and the choice will to some degree reflect the flavor of the oil as well as the strength and flavor of the acid—carefully balance it with the right amount of salt and pepper.

There are two vinaigrettes in this chapter—a basic vinaigrette, and a green sauce with an oil and vinegar base. They are excellent sauces and have a great many uses beyond dressing chicken.

BASIC VINAIGRETTE

❖❖❖

½ *cup oil*					*Salt*
About 1 *Tablespoon of freshly*		*Freshly ground black pepper*
   squeezed lemon juice or
   vinegar

Combine the oil, lemon juice or vinegar, and a little salt and pepper. Mix well and taste. Add more salt and pepper, if needed.

GREEN SAUCE

❖❖❖

This is a fantastic sauce, not only for warm or cold chicken but also for poached fish, steamed vegetables, and even for poached sausages like the Italian cotechino or the French garlic sausages. It takes little more than a few minutes of chopping to make; if you own a food processor, just throw everything in and let it make itself.

1 *cup good olive oil*			½ *cup chopped watercress*
2 *Tablespoons vinegar*			 *leaves*
1 *teaspoon Dijon mustard*		¼ *cup chopped fresh chives*
2 *Tablespoons capers, chopped*		 *or scallions, green part only*
2 *garlic cloves, finely chopped*		*Salt*
½ *cup chopped parsley*			*Freshly ground black pepper*

Combine all the ingredients except the salt and pepper, and mix well. Taste, and season with salt and pepper.

The final two sauces in this chapter are presented as bachelors because they are only called for once or twice in this book, and are used infrequently with chicken. Most cooks have a favorite recipe for tomato sauce, which they make often enough. But the basic brown sauce is a sauce many cooks shy away from because it is a bit of a production to make. The serious cook, however, should take the time to master it.

TOMATO SAUCE

———— ❖❖❖ ————

This recipe is well flavored with basil, which is a great complement to chicken.

6 *Tablespoons oil*
3 *garlic cloves, chopped*
2 *medium onions, chopped*
1 *1½- to 2-pound can Italian plum tomatoes* (about 1½ kilograms)
2 *12- to 14-ounce cans tomato purée* (about 350 grams each)

1 *teaspoon crushed dried thyme*
3 *Tablespoons crushed dried basil*
2 *teaspoons salt*
1 *teaspoon freshly ground black pepper*

Heat the oil in a large saucepan or pot over medium heat. When hot, add the garlic and onions, and sauté until tender and translucent but not browned, about 4 minutes. Add 1 tablespoon of the basil and the remaining ingredients and stir well, breaking up the large pieces of the whole tomatoes. Bring the sauce to a boil, then reduce the heat and simmer for 1 hour, stirring occasionally to prevent scorching.

Purée the sauce in a blender or food processor. Do this in a few batches, so as not to overfill the machine. Strain the sauce into a clean saucepan, and discard whatever bits of seed and pulp remain in the strainer.

Bring the sauce back to a boil, then reduce the heat and simmer for 30 to 60 minutes, until rich and thick in appearance. Stir frequently to prevent scorching. When the sauce has thickened as much as you would like, taste and adjust the seasonings. Add the other 2 tablespoons of crushed dried basil, and simmer for 5 minutes.

This sauce can be used immediately, or covered tightly and stored in the refrigerator or freezer.

Yield: 4 to 5 cups.

BASIC BROWN SAUCE

———— ❖❖❖ ————

As a general rule, chicken is accompanied by a white sauce or an egg-emulsion sauce. But occasionally chicken does call for the full, rich, deep flavor of a brown sauce.

3 *Tablespoons oil*
2 *cups miscellaneous chicken bones and giblets (but not livers)*
1 *small onion, peeled*
1 *small carrot*
½ *celery rib*
1 *garlic clove, unpeeled*
4 *Tablespoons butter*
4 *Tablespoons flour*

1 *quart rich, homemade, brown beef stock* (1 liter)
½ *cup red wine*
2 *ounces boiled ham* (50 grams)
3 *Tablespoons tomato purée or tomato sauce*
Salt
Freshly ground black pepper

Pour the oil into a large skillet over medium heat. When very hot, add the giblets and vegetables, and sauté until well browned on all sides. Transfer to a bowl, and set aside. Pour the oil out of the skillet, and add 3 to 4 tablespoons of water. Scrape all of the brown-encrusted bits on the bottom of the skillet into the rapidly evaporating water, and quickly pour this into the bowl with the giblets.

Melt the butter in a heavy saucepan over medium-low heat. When hot, add the flour and stir to form a smooth paste. This is a simple white roux. Continue to cook the roux over medium-low heat for 10 to 12 minutes, stirring frequently. First it will turn blond in color and become thin, then gradually it will darken until it is almost the color of milk chocolate. This is called a brown roux.

When the brown roux is ready, beat in the stock and wine. Add the giblets, vegetables, ham, and tomato purée or sauce. Bring the sauce to a boil over medium heat, stirring occasionally. Reduce the heat and simmer the sauce for 1 hour, skimming occasionally.

After the sauce has cooked for an hour, taste it. Adjust the seasoning by adding salt and pepper as needed. Simmer the sauce for 5 minutes longer, then pour through a strainer.

Yield: about 2 cups.

This sauce can be made well ahead of time, and safely stored for several days in the refrigerator, or several months in the freezer.

10

TRUSSING, BONING, AND CARVING

M

Y POULTERER is one of the best in the world. Unfortunately, a professional and caring butcher is very hard to find, so it is a good idea to learn to do some of the basic butchering techniques yourself.

Personally, I prefer to do most of my own butchering, but it really isn't necessary, since chicken can be purchased in most supermarkets already butchered. I do, however, believe you should learn to truss a bird yourself since you will often be instructed to truss the chicken in the middle of the recipe when the butcher isn't around. I also believe you should cut 2 or 3 chickens into serving pieces to learn a little about the anatomy of the bird. The difference between cutting a chicken into serving pieces when it's raw and carving it when it's cooked is small, and once you've cut up a couple of chickens, carving gracefully and elegantly at tableside will be amazingly easy.

TRUSSING

Trussing a chicken simply means tying the chicken so it holds its shape during cooking. Although it may look complicated in the diagram, it isn't. And once you get the knack of it, it only takes a few seconds. I learned this way of trussing from my butcher in New York, and it holds the chicken better than any of the more complicated trussing methods I have seen.

Place the chicken on its back, breast up, legs pointed toward you and the wings outstretched. Stretch the center of a 3-foot-long piece of string under the leg bones. Loop it around the legs, and cross it as it is pulled down between the legs. Now pull the strings around the tail and cross them underneath it. Tighten the string, which will pull the legs together and lift the tail to them.

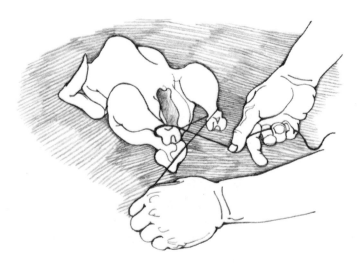

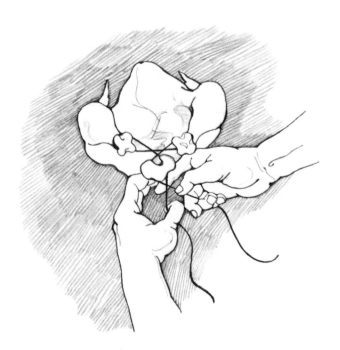

Next, pull the strings back, guiding them under the drumsticks. Just behind the drumsticks, press the string against the chicken with your thumbs, and flip the chicken over onto its breast, wings pointing toward you. Thread the strings through the wing, and pull together in a straight line across the back. The wings should be pressing firmly against the body. Check to see that the chicken is securely trussed before knotting.

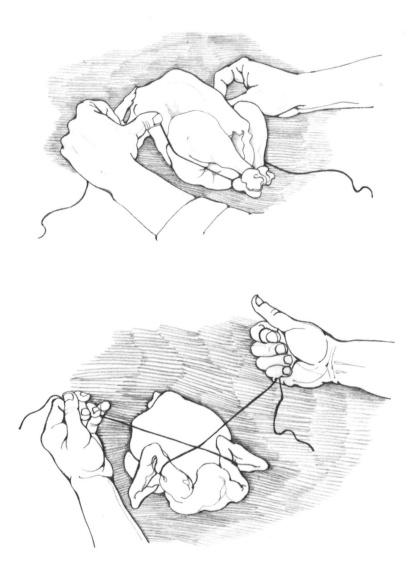

If you tie a double overhand knot and then twist the strings around, it will hold tight until the second knot is tied. A double overhand knot is just a simple knot like the one used for tying shoelaces, but the string is looped around itself twice instead of once. It is particularly useful when you're alone, as you don't need an extra hand to hold the first knot in place while the second is tied. After knotting, cut off any excess string.

Pull the neck flap around to the back and tuck under the string. Tuck the wings over the neck flap. The chicken is now trussed.

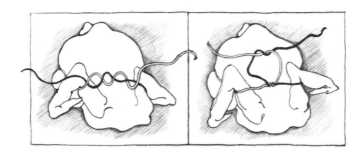

CUT INTO SERVING PIECES*

"Cut into serving pieces" simply means cutting the chicken into 10 pieces—2 legs, 2 thighs, 2 wings, 2 half-breasts, and the back split in two.

THE LEGS AND THIGHS: Place the chicken on its back, breast up, and legs pointed toward you. Press the leg and thigh on one side of the chicken outward from the body until the skin between the thigh and the body is taut. Pierce the skin with the point of a sharp knife, then cut through it in an arc to expose

---

* Chicken can be purchased already cut into pieces in most markets. Feel free to substitute any combination of chicken pieces in recipes calling for chicken "cut into serving pieces."

the inside of the thigh, pressing firmly down on the leg as you go. This releases the leg and thigh from the skin holding it to the body. Repeat with the leg and thigh on the other side of the body.

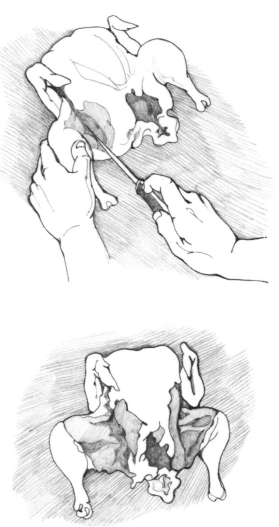

Next, grasp the legs in your hands, with your thumbs firmly pressing against the thigh bone. Lift the chicken and bend the leg-thigh pieces down and under the chicken until the end of the thigh bone pops out of the hip joint and is clearly exposed.

Place the chicken back on the counter, and beginning at the far end of the thigh, cut through the dark meat at the base of the back and continue through the exposed hip joint and along the backbone until the leg and thigh is removed. Remove the other leg and thigh in exactly the same way.

Now separate the legs from the thighs: lift one of the pieces, move the bones around, and locate the joint in the middle. With the point of the knife, make a small cut through the meat to expose the joint. If you are slightly to the right or left of the joint, relocate the joint, and again make a small cut in the meat to expose it. When the joint is clearly exposed, cut completely

through it to separate the leg from the thigh. If you are finding it hard to cut, it means you are cutting into the bone. Either persevere and continue cutting through the bone, or cut through more of the meat around the joint; grasping the leg in one hand and the thigh in the other, bend them back until the leg bone pops out of the knee joint and you can see exactly where to cut.

Separate the other leg and thigh in the same way.

THE WINGS: Locate the shoulder joint where the wing connects to the breast. Move the wing around to make sure you know where the joint is located. With a sharp knife make a small cut through the skin and flesh to expose the joint. With the pointed end of the knife, pierce through the joint and cut around the end of the wing to remove it, cutting off as little of the breast as possible. Repeat with the other wing.

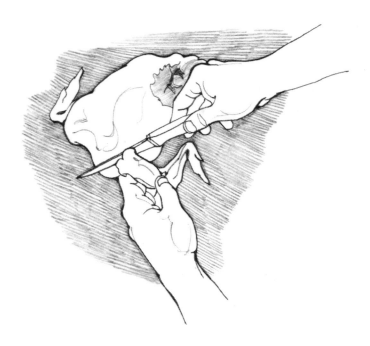

For sautéing and broiling or grilling, I usually cut off the wing tip. While this is not essential, the wing will color better and cook more evenly if it is removed.

To REMOVE THE WING TIP: Place the wing flat on the counter. Locate the first joint, which can almost be seen through the thin layer of skin and meat that covers it, and cut through it. Repeat with the other wing. Save the wing tip for stock.

To SEPARATE THE BREAST AND BACK: Stand the body of the chicken on its neck end. At the top is a thin sheathing that leads down to cover the rib cage. There is a thin line of fat that forms a natural curve along the bottom of the breast. Pierce the sheathing with the point of the knife, and cut downward right through the ribs and into the neck opening. The knife should follow the natural curve of the thin line of fat, cutting just under it so that all the flesh remains on the breast. Turn the chicken around and repeat on the other side.

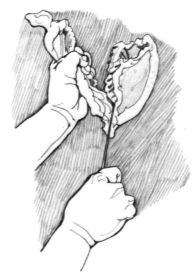

Place the breast, skin side down, on the counter. With a large cook's knife, cut it in half lengthwise. It may be necessary to rap on the top of the knife, or to use a slight chopping movement initially, to cut through the bones.

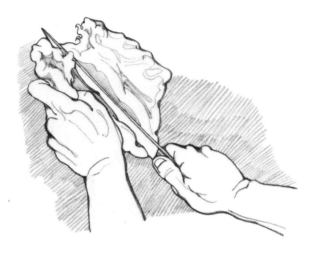

I like to remove the split breastbones now so that the breast will cook more evenly and color better. With the tip of a small, pointed knife, cut through the transparent membrane that covers the bones along the edge of the white cartilage and around the hard center disc of the breastbone. Do not cut into the flesh. Put the knife down, and slide your fingers along the disc and cartilage, separating the flesh from the bone. Holding the meat of the breast firmly on the counter, pull the bones out. (See pages 232–33.)

THE BACK: Using a heavy cook's knife or cleaver, chop the back horizontally in half (for serving), or into 4 or 5 pieces (for making stock).

BONING A CHICKEN BREAST

Place the breast on a counter, skin side down. Look at the skeletal chart, and then at the breast. Move your fingers around the breast until you feel familiar with the location of the various bones. Now turn the breast skin side up.

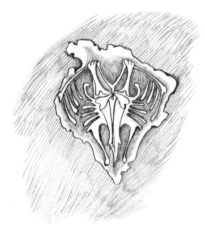

First remove the skin. Grasp the skin firmly in your hand by the excess flap at the neck end. With your other hand, press the breast firmly onto the counter, and pull the skin off. If slippery, hold it in a kitchen towel.

Next, locate the wishbone.

Look at the skeletal chart. Press your fingers against the flesh until you feel the wishbone. Using the tip of a sharp, pointed knife, make a small cut along the length of the wishbone. Loosen

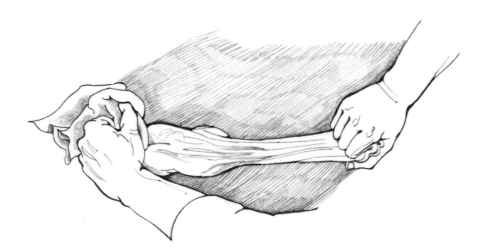

the meat from the bone with your fingers. With the tip of the knife, cut around the meat at the ends of the wishbone, and twist and pull it out.

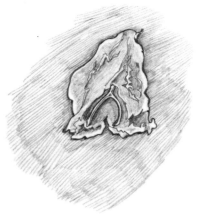

The breast should still be skin side up. With the heel of your hand, push down firmly on the ridge of the breastbone until you hear it crunch. Lift the breast into your hand, placing your thumbs on either side of the breastbone, with the rest of your hand supporting the breast from underneath. Bend the breast downward until the breastbone pops up.

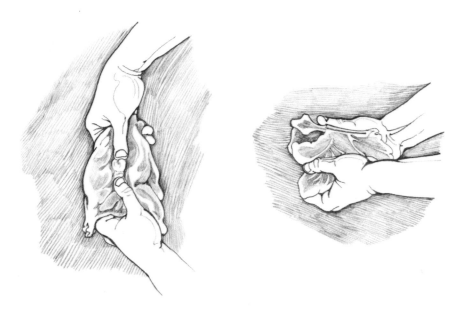

Place the breast flat on the counter, and with the tip of the knife, pierce just through the thin, white sheathing along the sides of the breastbone and down along the white cartilage. This is meant to only cut through the sheathing, not to cut out the bone. Slide your finger along the bone to release the flesh from the bone and the white cartilage. Holding the upper part of the breast firmly on the counter with one hand, grab the top of the breastbone with the other hand and pull it out. Both the hard disc of the breastbone and the white cartilage should come out in one piece. If broken, hold the breast firmly on the counter and pull out the piece.

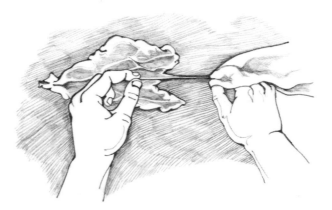

Next, slide the point of the knife under the collarbone, and pulling upward as you go, carefully cut it out. Slide your fingers under the few remaining rib bones and lift them off.

On the underside of the meat you willl see 2 long, thin, white tendons. Slide the point of your knife under the end of the tendon, and cut enough of it free to grasp it between your fingers. Wrap a kitchen towel around the end of the tendon, and grasp firmly. With your other hand, use 2 fingers to squeeze against the exposed tendon, and squeezing very hard, pull the tendon through your fingers. The tendon should come out in one piece, free of any meat. Release the other tendon in the same way.

For suprêmes: The breast is now fully boned. To make it into 2 chicken suprêmes, simply cut it in half lengthwise.

TO SPLIT A CHICKEN DOWN THE BACK

Hold the chicken so that the neck end is pressing against the counter, the pope's nose pointing up in the air, and the backbone facing you. With a sharp, sturdy kitchen knife or poultry shears, begin cutting just under the pope's nose, and cut all the way down along the edge of the backbone so that the chicken is split from stem to stern. Holding the chicken in basically the same position as before but grasping it firmly to hold it together, cut down along the other edge of the backbone, the same way as before, and remove it. Save for stock.

Place the chicken on the counter, skin side humping upward, and press down firmly on the breast with the palm of your hand. You will hear a few of the small bones crack, and the chicken will be resting flat on the counter. Turn the chicken skin side down.

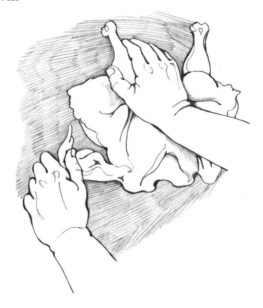

In the center of the breast is a disc-shaped, dark bone with a long piece of white cartilage running from the center of the chicken to the tip of the breast. You will also notice a thin, almost transparent membrane covering the bones. With the tip

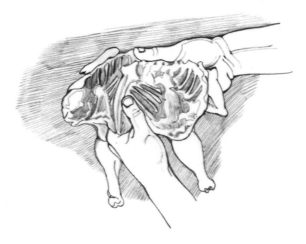

of a sharp knife, cut just barely through the membrane around the breastbone and down both sides of the cartilage. Do not pierce into the meat—all that needs cutting is the thin sheathing.

Pick the chicken up in your hands, and bend it downward so that the breastbone protrudes clearly. Place the chicken on the counter, skin side down, and press one hand squarely and firmly above the protruding breastbone. With the other hand, pull out the breastbone, pulling in the direction of the white cartilage. If the entire length of the cartilage does not come out with the breastbone, slide your finger around the broken pieces to loosen the flesh clinging to them, and pull it out.

That's it. Turn the chicken over again, tuck the wings under, and press the legs against either side of the breast.

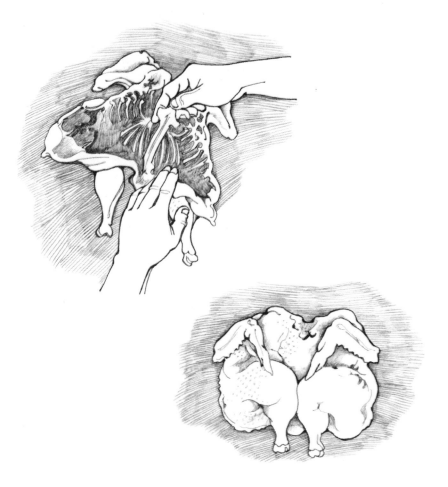

TO CUT A CHICKEN
IN HALF FOR BAKING

Slit the chicken as directed above; then, with a sharp cook's knife, cut vertically through the breast, splitting the chicken into two halves.

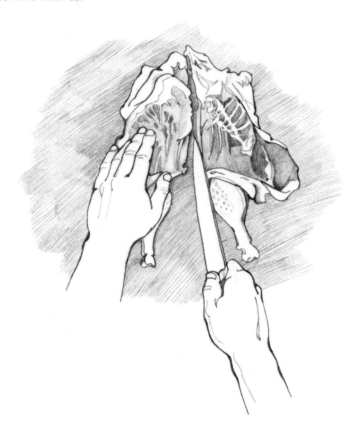

CHINESE CHICKEN WINGS

I first saw this technique demonstrated by a Chinese chef in San Francisco. It's not terribly difficult, but it is a very time-consuming chore. If you need 24 for a party, plan on spending the better part of an afternoon boning wings.

With a small, sharp, pointed knife, cut off the wing tip of the first joint (see illustration on page 227). Save for stock. The wing will now have 2 remaining sections—one with 2 bones in it, the other with a single larger bone. You want to bring all of the meat and skin to the center joint and remove the 2 bones, leaving a ball of meat on the end of the single larger bone.

Cut around all the skin and meat at the end of the 2 bones. Make certain that the skin, meat, and tendons are loosened all around. Now, holding the end of the two bones in one hand,

use the fingers of your other hand to push the meat down the bones as though you were peeling off a glove, inside out. As you reach the joint, it may be necessary to scrape with your knife. Always keep the edge of the knife against the bone to ensure that even if you do slip, you will not pierce through the flesh or skin. When you can clearly see the joint, cut off the 2 bones. Save these for stock.

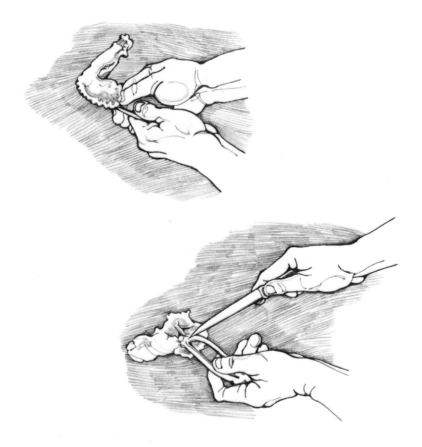

Repeat basically the same procedure on the other side. Cut around the top of the bone, releasing all the meat, skin, and tendons from the end of the bone. With the edge of your knife, begin scraping the meat down the bone. As soon as you have scraped enough of the meat clear of the top to grip it, hold it in one hand, and slide your fingers down along the bone, again in the same fashion as before, as though you were removing a glove inside out, scraping with the edge of your knife when necessary. Gently press the meat from the other section into the center of the meat coming down from the larger bone, and shape into a ball.

CARVING

Small chickens should be carved in half, medium-sized birds in quarters, and large chickens or capons in quarters with the breast cut into several pieces.

CARVING A CHICKEN
IN HALF

THE LEGS AND THIGHS: Arrange the chicken in the center of the carving board or platter, breast up. With a fork, gently press one of the legs down toward the platter until the skin that connects the thigh to the body is taut. Cut through the skin that holds the leg and thigh in place. Press the leg and thigh downward onto the platter until the joint that connects it to the carcass is exposed. Pierce through the joint, and cut off the leg and thigh. Set it aside, and remove the other leg and thigh the same way.

All that remains is to remove the two wings, and then the breast.

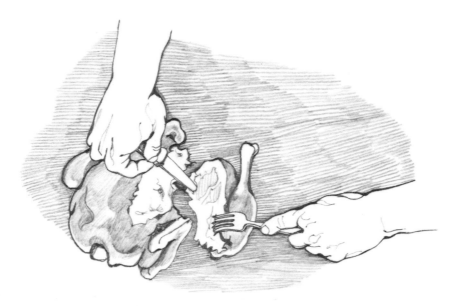

THE WINGS: Make a small cut through the skin and meat around the shoulder joint, where the wing connects to the carcass. Carefully press downward on the wing to expose the joint. With the tip of a pointed knife, pierce through the shoulder joint and cut off the wing. Cut off as little of the breast meat as possibe when removing the wing. Repeat with the other wing.

THE BREAST: Press a fork firmly into the base or backbone to hold the bird securely in place. With the tip of the knife, pierce deeply through the skin and the meat, just to one side of the ridge at the top of the breast formed by the protruding breast-

bone. Cut down until you feel the knife pressing against the bones. Holding the chicken secure with the fork, cut through the skin and meat the full length of the breast, from one end of the chicken to the other. Insert the fork into the top of the breast and begin lifting the breast off the bones, using the tip

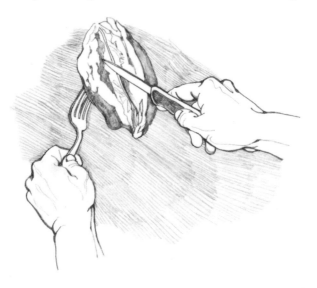

of the knife to loosen any bits of meat which adhere to the carcass. Turn the chicken around, and remove the other half breast in exactly the same way.

Each portion consists of one wing, one half breast, and one leg and thigh.

QUARTERING A CHICKEN

Quartering a chicken is basically the same as halving it. The only difference is that the legs and thighs are disjointed, and the breast pieces are cut in half horizontally.

To quarter a chicken, carve it in half as directed above.

Place the leg and thigh piece on the platter or carving board, skin side down. With the tip of the knife, pierce deeply into the knee joint. If you miss, try again. When you are certain that you have located the knee joint, cut through it and separate the leg from the thigh. Repeat with the other leg and thigh.

Place each piece of breast on the platter, skin side down. Cut it horizontally in half.

The chicken has now been carved in quarters. Each portion consists of one leg or thigh and one piece of the breast. Reserve the wings for anyone wanting seconds.

FOR LARGE CHICKENS
OR CAPONS

Carve the chicken into quarters, but cut each half-breast into 3 or 4 slices on the bias. Portions might consist of just a leg or a thigh, or a few pieces of the breast, or a combination of light and dark meat. The wing from a large chicken has a lot of meat on it, so do not feel embarrassed to serve it.

INDEX

ABOUT THE AUTHOR

*Carl Jerome was Director of The James Beard
Cooking Classes and faculty member of The Good Cooking School.
He is co-author with James Beard of* Cuisinart Food Processor Cookbook,
and one of the hosts in The Bloomingdale's Book of Entertainment.
*He recently returned to the United States after living in London
for two years, and resides in New York.*